DATE DUE

PRINTED IN U.S.A.

OTHER TITLES OF INTEREST FROM ST. LUCIE PRESS

7 Secrets of Successful Sales Management

Total Quality in Marketing

The Seven Fatal Management Sins

The High Cost of Low Morale...and What to Do About It

Management Golf

The Motivating Team Leader

Skills of Encouragement: Bringing Out the Best in Yourself and Others

The New Leader: Bringing Creativity and Innovation to the Workplace

Inner Self, Outer Self

For more information about these titles call, fax or write:

St. Lucie Press
2000 Corporate Blvd., N.W.
Boca Raton, FL 33431-9868

TEL (561) 994-0555 • (800) 272-7737
FAX (800) 374-3401
E-MAIL information@slpress.com
WEB SITE http://www.slpress.com

S$\overset{t}{\text{L}}$

High-Impact Sales Force Automation

A Strategic Perspective

High-Impact Sales Force Automation

A Strategic Perspective

Glen S. Petersen

S_L^t

St. Lucie Press
Boca Raton, Florida

Phone: (561) 994-0555
E-mail: information@slpress.com
Web site: http://www.slpress.com

S^t_L

Published by
St. Lucie Press
2000 Corporate Blvd., N.W.
Boca Raton, FL 33431-9868

CONTENTS

PREFACE

Since its inception in the early to mid-1980s, sales force automation has been the subject of a whirlwind of controversy. The industry has grown out of a few technology-based start-up companies. Because the early adopters consisted of major Fortune 500 companies, these early installs drew considerable attention from the business community. One of the primary issues was concern regarding the potential for an adequate rate of return given other non-system-based investments. In many respects, this questioning was appropriate because functionality was truly limited and applications targeted administrative tasks. However, from a long-term perspective, these early adopters were learning how to utilize a technology that is quickly becoming a competitive necessity; further, their sales force was establishing the discipline and orientation that would allow it to quickly adapt to new technology and platforms as they became available.

Another confusing factor was the use of the term *sales force automation.* Use of the technology does not "automate" the sales force; it can, however, automate portions of processes, and it definitely forces discipline in handling transactions and data. Unfortunately, the term "automation" has been equated to automatic or easy results by some of the early adopters, and this led their organizations to failure.

Given that early focus was on the capabilities of technology, it is not surprising that early installs were often championed by the IS organization rather than the line organization. The result was expensive technology that no one used. Observing these situations, suppliers quickly discovered that success required a team approach involving both IS and the sales organization. It also became readily apparent to the suppliers that customers needed a host of services such as system operation, training, help-line support, hardware replacement, etc. Although this was a welcome source of revenue, it did require a rapid ramp-up of infrastructure. Over time, it was recognized that successful installs required a fairly complex combination of end-user focus, plus an appropriate combination of systems capabilities and services. This recipe for success remains essentially true today, but with the complexity of options available today, more discipline is required to keep the project on track.

With over 600 suppliers of "sales force automation software" and many choices of devices and communication medium, the current market can be characterized as diverse and fractious. A clear indication of complexity is the emergence of services that help one navigate through the many software and service providers. This situation is further complicated by the speed of change within the technology. Prospective end-user organizations are dealing with a constantly moving target accentuated by a constant barrage of announcements regarding new capabilities (or planned capabilities). There is little reason to assume that this situation is going to change anytime soon. Thus, decisions regarding hardware and software will be difficult unless the user organization has a very good definition of where it wants go and how to get there.

The fast pace of change within the technology arena is being closely matched by changes in the business environment. Global competition has accentuated the importance of "time" as a critical and non-renewable resource. Misuse of this resource can be competitively fatal. Just-in-time manufacturing and compression of time to market are becoming the commonly accepted norm. Another indication of the speed with which change is occurring is the realization that the basic business model from which an organization operates can become obsolete in a matter of a few years. Examples of this are IBM and Microsoft (as it reacts to the threat of the Internet). Similarly, companies that historically depended on economies of scale as a competitive barrier find their base being eroded by smaller, more flexible competitors. The issue here is that the foundation of competitiveness within industries can change, not in decades, but in a few years. Thus, management today involves a need for constant vigilance and emphasis on increasing speed and value.

The relevance of this complexity and rate of change to the sales function is that it must adapt to meet the needs of the competitive environment. The good news is that a properly designed and configured sales force automation system can:

■ Reduce cycle times for customer-focused processes

■ Reduce waste

■ Add value to the customer

■ Leverage competitiveness in the marketplace.

These capabilities do not occur automatically; they must be planned and integrated into the overall system.

To maximize the impact of technology applied to the sales function, it should be apparent that the technology must be approached **as a part of a solution** and not as an end unto itself. To truly leverage an investment in sales force automation requires a market- (customer-) driven perspective regarding the desired competitive needs of the sales force; otherwise, technology will merely reflect current processes, and any returns will essentially be based on gains in efficiency. The focus of this competitive evaluation must be on the end user (salesperson) and the customer. What is the customer's (and/or prospect's) business and how do they compete in their marketplace? The parallel question, then, is how can the salesperson add value to the customer and effectively maintain or sell into the account? Given the desirability of leveraging the customer base, the salespeople are going to have relevance only to the extent to which they contribute to the needs of that organization. Technology can leverage these capabilities, but hiring practices, structure, incentives, etc. all play a part in behavior in the field.

Today's systems technology is capable of supporting a wide variety of sophisticated applications. The challenge is rapidly becoming one of being disciplined in limiting the technology rather than technology being the limiting factor. Without a solid business perspective, there is a very real danger of applications becoming technology driven, and this situation is highly correlated with poor return on investment and field frustration.

This book is based on over ten years of experience within the sales automation industry. During this time, the author has experienced the industry as an end user, as a vendor of sales automation software and services, and as a consultant. The recommendations and comments are based on what has historically worked and not worked. The book is not intended to be a step-by-step methodology. Rather, it presents a perspective regarding issues and how to tie these into a course of action that will prove to be successful from a business point of view.

One of the key motivations for writing the book was to communicate the need for strategic input to the sales automation process from senior management. There has been a historical tendency by senior management to approach sales force automation as a "back office" application of technology. In so doing, senior management has often delegated a decision process that should command more personal attention. Most guidelines for sales automation cite senior management support, but what is really needed is senior management involvement and understanding. The implementation of sales force automation inevitably involves trade-offs; senior management needs to be aware of the implications of key decisions so that they can effectively lead, while allowing the implementation team to manage the process.

Acknowledgments

The idea of writing a book regarding sales force automation has been a desire of mine since I was first introduced to the technology. At that time, the capabilities were rudimentary, but I was struck by the tremendous potential to leverage the efforts of the sales function and the organization as a whole.

The concept for the book is a culmination of research and practical experience in the field. I am indebted to Todd Scofield and Dean Herington, Jr. of Princeton Strategic Partners, Inc. for their feedback and suggestions regarding the methodologies discussed in the book. My special thanks go to Ralph Smith of Occidental Chemical Company, who provided encouragement and edited drafts of the book.

This book builds upon and synthesizes many ideas of other writers in the fields of sales, general management, quality, strategy, and customer service. I have tried to acknowledge my sources closely throughout the text. Credit is due to these leaders in their respective disciplines. I am also, of course, grateful to my clients, who have helped me shape and refine my ideas regarding strategy and sales force automation. In no case does this book contain data that have not been obtained from public sources.

Last, but most importantly, for her tolerance and understanding when I was writing instead of attending to her needs, I thank my wife Melinda.

ABOUT THE AUTHOR

Glen S. Petersen is the President and founder of Strategic Sales Performance, Inc., a sales force automation consulting firm that focuses on conducting needs assessments for Fortune 1000 companies. Prior to his involvement with sales force automation, Mr. Petersen did strategic planning for companies in diverse industries such as electronics, pharmaceuticals, and the food industry. During this period, he interfaced with sales, marketing, manufacturing, and finance. Through this experience, he developed a keen sense of the potential for synergy among these functions.

In 1982, he was recruited by M&M/Mars to manage the development of sales performance tools for the company. This led to the design and development of a sales force automation project. The system was fully deployed in 1987, and, in 1988, Mr. Petersen joined Sales Technologies, Inc., a venture capital-based provider of sales force automation software and services. From this perspective, he learned the challenges of growing a technology-based company while reinvesting in future platform releases. He also observed how many companies from diverse industries approach sales force automation.

Having experienced the industry from the end-user and vendor perspectives, Mr. Petersen became an independent consultant and, in 1993, co-founded a sales force automation consulting company that offered both needs assessment and system development and integration capabilities.

Mr. Petersen has written many articles on sales force automation and has been a speaker at sales automation events and trade shows. He holds master's degrees in engineering and business from the Illinois Institute of Technology and the University of Chicago, respectively. For more information regarding Mr. Petersen and other materials he has written, contact the Strategic Sales Performance, Inc. web site at salesperformance.com.

CHAPTER 1

A STRATEGIC PERSPECTIVE

The Need for a New Perspective

The sales force automation industry is over ten years old. Many of the original innovators in the industry have faded while numerous start-up companies have taken their place. The industry consists of a vast array of hardware suppliers, shrink-wrapped products, software application specialties, communications software specialists, accessory manufacturers, systems integrators, and consultants of various size and specialization. It is a complex, competitive arena in and for user organizations to navigate. Despite the explosion in hardware and software technology, the industry retains a focus on productivity and cost reduction. In this context, there has been an on-going debate regarding the balance of end-user (sales rep) needs vs. organizational needs. Historically, the needs of the two groups have been viewed as largely antagonistic to one another. Due to the historical limitations in systems technology, systems have largely evolved as end-user driven or organizationally driven.

Current technology allows for the ability to balance system applications so that both end-user and organizational needs are met. However, if organizational needs take on a command and control management style, the system assumes the vestige of a tug-of-war, where there is tension and a sense of win/lose. This book advocates using a broader context of delivering value to the customer. If an organization uses as its focus performance relative to the customer, the system becomes a win/ win/win (sales rep, organization, customer). A strategic approach that is based on value will drive the organization to support the sales organization and will motivate salespeople to honor their commitments to the customer and to the organization as a whole. The result will be increases in revenue and margin that are accompanied by reduction in cost and cycle time. It is time for a new paradigm that is consistent with the needs of the marketplace (i.e., looking for solutions to companies' competitive needs).

This book is intended to address issues experienced by end-user organizations and the suppliers of sales automation software and services. With this objective in mind, each chapter provides a perspective that will be relevant to both groups. This book is dedicated to business issues and solutions. There are other sources of detailed "how to" and technology-based materials that will assist organizations in the course of implementing their projects. The remainder of this chapter will address the historical evolution of the industry. It is always easier to understand the current situation if you know how you got there.

The industry tends to segment solutions into three categories:

- Fully networked systems that are integrated with other corporate systems.

- Fully networked systems that are essentially stand-alone.

- Non-networked systems that are comprised of essentially personal productivity tools.

Since the thrust of this book is directed at the integration of organizational effort behind the sales efforts of the organization, the majority of the concepts and discussion will be oriented toward networked systems.

From its inception, the industry has been pushed and pulled regarding cost, performance, and economic viability. Anecdotal evidence suggests glorious results while surveys tend to give sales automation questionable performance marks. Perhaps due to the number of suppliers/ products in the sales automation market today and the confusion regarding system platform and organizational "fit," there has never been more seminars or more seminar participants than in today's market. Clearly, there is a high level of interest; however, is the need (solution orientation) being effectively defined and fulfilled?

The sales force automation industry essentially provides a set of technologically based tools that must fit in a corporate context for its customers. These customers must put into place sophisticated and integrated systems that retain relevance and effectiveness in the face of galloping changes in technology and competitiveness. Moreover, they must install a complex technology in an operating environment (sales) that is notoriously difficult to manage yet fundamental to the success of the corporation as a whole. The issues are obviously greater than technology.

The content of this book will attempt to provide a user-oriented context for the design and implementation of networked and integrated sales force automation systems. It is meant to be directional in nature and is intended to be a reference for sales force automation suppliers, project team members, and senior management. The foundation of the book is built on Peter Drucker's admonition, "There is only one valid definition of business purpose: to create a customer."[1]

The method and approach advocated in this book positions sales force automation as a set of tools that facilitate the delivery of value to the supplier's customer. The book presents sales automation in the context of business needs, as an enabling technology; when projects leave this context, they are headed for trouble.

This chapter will set the stage for the remainder of the book. It will trace the evolution of the industry and suggest a future path for both sales force automation suppliers and end-user organizations.

Emergence of the Industry

During the high growth eras of the 50s and 60s, sales organizations essentially followed the growth curves of corporate revenue. Even in the 70s when American industry began to seriously examine productivity performance, the sales function was largely excluded from serious consideration. In the late 70s, technology started to appear that had the potential to reduce the administrative burden associated with managing the sales force. With softening demand and ever increasing costs, many industries were ready to try technology that offered a way to reduce cost, and reporting turnaround time, while increasing accountability.

For many companies, the major indicators of sales productivity are sales costs as a percent of total revenue dollars. Other companies augment this type of information with call reports, which are often considered a surrogate index of sales effort. While call reporting was viewed as a necessary barometer of sales activity and market status, it was recognized that the process was expensive and provided data that was less than actionable. Certainly, as a sales budget item, the call reporting and status reporting processes stood out as a prime target for cost reduction. Desire to improve a process and the ability to do so can be two widely separate propositions. At one end of the spectrum was hand consolidation of the data, while at the other end was keying data into a system. Neither system was appealing from a cost or timeliness perspective. Due to the peak and valley nature of the input, it was obvious that the work might be better handled via an outsourcing arrangement. As optical reader and electrical sensing equipment became available, these technologies were deployed; thus, the call report consisted of filling in dots as opposed to writing. These techniques were flawed in several important capabilities:

■ As a command and control tool, was it really relevant (actionable)?

■ Despite the technology, there was a significant delay in processing the data and generating reports. Typical delay was 4–6 weeks. Field delay was often 6–8 weeks.

■ When errors or incomplete data were reported, did the system provide a means for correcting the data? How much productive time was lost, and how much delay was associated with the correction process?

■ How much error did the process itself introduce?

■ Reports typically consisted of enough paper to fill a room.

In addition to the question of timeliness, these systems also challenged the question of who owns the data. If there is a question regarding completeness and/or accuracy, is the data ignored, does the administrator guess, or is the question handed back to the field, thereby delaying reports? Thus, it was difficult to lift the data out of the realm of political contention.

As computer technology began to emerge, palm-sized programmable devices came on the market. These "hand-held" devices had limited functionality and keyboard functions, but they could be used for call reporting and simple order entry. In their initial form, the devices supported only one-way communication; thus, they had the ability to speed reporting, but as changes and updates were required, the units had to be returned to a central location for physical reprogramming. Despite these limitations, these devices were used by companies that either sought to reduce costs or needed market-level data faster than could be supported by means of paper-based systems.

Where keyboard functions were more important, clipboard devices with one-line LCD screens and portable terminals emerged to address field needs. Portable terminals were essentially used for rudimentary E-mail while the clipboard devices were the equivalent of hand-helds.

In the mid-80s, true laptop computers became available. A handful of innovators grasped the significance of the full computer functionality and developed proprietary systems that were completely dedicated to field sales requirements. Of particular significance was the ability to communicate in a two-way manner and actually update remote user systems using the communication capability. Thus, the laptop computer had the ability to avoid the pitfalls of previous technologies and speed processing in a manner not possible with paper-based systems.

Focus on Productivity

The business cycles of the 1970s spurred a corporate emphasis on productivity and cost reduction. As these initiatives matured, the productivity perspective spread from manufacturing to all functional groups and the corporation at large. Toward the latter part of the decade, Total Quality Management (TQM) started to acquire visibility as an important contributor to cost reduction and competitiveness. At the same time, information systems (IS) organizations had largely automated "back room" processes and were in a position to expand into other functional areas. The sales and marketing areas tended to be shunned by IS due to the quagmire of open-ended and constantly shifting needs. It was not uncommon for sales and marketing to outsource their systems needs (e.g., call reporting). Thus, in the mid-80s with the emphasis still on cost reduction and new technologies emerging to address the needs of sales and marketing, the stage was set for organizations to pioneer the application of sales force automation.

From a vendor perspective, this confluence of needs and capabilities had the traits of an ideal niche market: a large population of end users, pent-up demand (need recognized), and specialized needs that would be unattractive to major software houses. Given the limitations of the early laptop computers and the interest in reducing administrative costs and improving productivity, the obvious choice was to develop applications that had the following characteristics:

- Addressed the standard administrative needs of most sales forces.

- Could be modified to meet the specific look and functionality desired by the customer without changing core logic.

- Provided a means for communicating data and information (two-way) from the field to corporate and from corporate to the field.

- Had development costs which could be maintained at a level that would equate to a reasonable set of license costs and break-even points relative to in-house development.

- Could provide reasonable functionality given the limited hardware memory and DOS capabilities at that time.

Thus, the SFA industry, which lent itself to administrative and reporting functions, was "birthed" during an era of emphasis on productivity, while still facing severe technological challenges.

Problems Emerge Early

From a vendor standpoint, the sales automation sale was a missionary sales process. With few benchmarks and fewer standards, it was truly a pioneering effort for the vendor and the customer. Customers (or prospects) always wanted to stretch the functionality of the applications or to add new applications. This pressure to stretch or expand functionality placed significant resource and financial demands on the vendors. The pressure was positive in that it pulled the industry along, but there was always a temptation to take risks that had a bad habit of appearing at the wrong time. To effectively address the communication and reporting needs of their client base, suppliers had to adopt a "suite" of applications. These applications varied by supplier, but they included E-mail, call reporting, territory management, rudimentary spreadsheets, and reports distribution. Order entry tended to be a specialty due to its unique characteristics. There was a sense of "critical mass" from the start of the new industry (i.e., sufficient capability to equate to financial return for the organization and sufficient functionality to make sense to the field sales organization). Vendors had to develop a reasonable suite of applications to be viable.

The suite of applications had both asset and liability traits. On the one hand, the suite was an almost necessary part of being in the business at all; however, as hardware and operating system technology moved from faltering steps to a full gallop, upgrading the full suite of products became an operational impossibility. Given a business model that uses license fees to pay for sunk costs, as well as to finance future development, the constant need to upgrade and modify became a financial drain, and some companies never were able to convert the process into a profitable operation. The other aspect of this conversion process was the parallel effort to upgrade internal training and installation processes to keep up with the change. In retrospect, these difficulties were almost trivial compared to the platform shifts and options that have occurred over the past few years. The resources required to update and upgrade a complete suite of applications and always be current with available technology is a daunting proposition and cannot serve as a model for the future.

From the customer perspective, there was an early perception that applying this technology was the same as any systems project. Thus, IS organizations directed and essentially controlled many of the early installs. One aspect of this approach was that vendors were selected on the basis of system platform choices rather than the appropriateness of the application. The second error was to assume that technical people could design the system and that salespeople would just use it. The third danger was the tendency to become enamored with the technology. This was so prevalent in the early stages of the industry that the phrase "It's not the laptop, Stupid!" was coined. As experience with projects grew, vendors and observers of the industry began to identify critical success factors associated with what had been considered "successful" installs. These admonitions took on the form of the ten do's (or don'ts) of sales force automation. Though the lists varied somewhat by source, they essentially covered the following points:

1. Gain top management support.

2. Seek early wins with reps.

3. Create a multi-disciplined team.

4. Introduce applications that work the way the rep works.

5. Address applications that the sales organization feels are a priority.

6. Involve field salespeople in the design.

7. Pilot test all applications with clear success criteria.

8. Use quality training and invest in adequate training time.

9. Provide superior field support–minimize problems.

10. Have a clear champion for the system.

These points remain relevant today and are periodically referenced within the industry and in related publications.

Despite the growing evidence of "success" and the continued improvement in application design, many consultants questioned the sales force automation investment based on the limited scope of the capabilities and the opportunity cost to invest those resources elsewhere. For example, some professionals suggested that productivity objectives could be obtained equally through improved hiring and training. Others pointed out the need for improved deployment and targeting of reps. Others cited the lack of sales tools. Thus, the professional ranks considered the "jury to be out" regarding sales force automation.

An exception to this skepticism was the pharmaceutical industry. This industry became one of the early adopters of sales force automation. There were several reasons for this advocacy.

■ Research had demonstrated a high correlation between call patterns on doctors with high prescription rates and ultimate product demand.

■ Demand for product is virtually totally a function of the effectiveness of the sales force to position the product and create trial usage.

■ Market share for new products was typically established by market penetration achieved during the first six months after product introduction.

■ Pharmaceutical reps have high compensation packages.

■ The industry is highly networked; therefore, success in one area tends to be known quickly.

One of the capabilities of the early systems was territory management. This application provided a better means to prepare for calls and to plan coverage to meet certain call pattern criteria. The applications also helped reps to adapt their coverage when they encountered delays or doctors not being available. These efforts had enormous leverage. Ciba-Geigy reported that a 1% increase in productivity generated a 6.7% increase in revenue. Success in this area spread to other industries and helped the industry grow at a faster rate than it might otherwise have experienced.

A Watershed Article

At the beginning of 1989, two Harvard Business School professionals published an article in the *Harvard Business Review* regarding sales and marketing systems (widely interpreted as sales force automation).[2] Beyond the legitimacy afforded by having the topic discussed in "the journal," the authors cited conclusions that continue to be quoted in the industry today (sales increases of 10–30%+ and investment returns of over 100%). As a matter of fact, the subtitle for the article is "Productivity gets a lift from information technology." To reinforce this productivity orientation, Moriarity and Swartz noted:

■ Direct labor has been reduced to the level of **8–12% of production costs** in manufacturing companies.

■ Sales and marketing costs average **15–35% of total corporate costs**.

In addition, the article identified many successful installs to back up its claims. From a productivity and cost reduction perspective, the article clearly delineated sales and marketing as a fruitful area for systems investment. For the sales force automation industry, the article represented a new "launch pad" to establish viability and gain access to top management.

Despite the reference to productivity and return on investment, the Moriarity and Swartz article had a significantly greater scope than sales force automation:

1. Throughout the entire article, the authors refer to marketing and sales productivity "MSP" systems. Thus, they were addressing **the integrated needs** of sales and marketing.

2. The authors quote the National Association of Accountants' findings that manufacturers' **service activities account for 75–85% of all value added**.

3. Integration and management of distribution channels is referenced repeatedly, particularly in the context of marketing database functions.

4. The authors' definition of guiding steps included the following:

   ■ View the project scope from a corporate standpoint (reference to **linkage,** not user interface).

   ■ "Concentrate on tasks that can **add value** for the customer."

   ■ "Modify the technology and the organization to support the system." Essentially this is a dual admonition. Employ technology as an enabler rather than as a driver. Don't automate flawed systems.

   ■ Seek competitive advantage (look beyond economy or productivity to impact).

■ The concluding remarks provide a warning to avoid overselling the capabilities of the technology in the context of representing it as a "silver bullet" (not the term used by the authors). Technology cannot rectify poorly developed marketing programs or ineffective processes.

The article gave impetus to the industry, provided input for top management consideration, and could have provided direction for the industry. However, as will be explained in the next section, the industry appears to be caught in the productivity mind-set.

As was outlined earlier, the constant migration of technology has caused the sales automation software vendors to upgrade their applications to keep pace; this has resulted in applications with greater depth and improved user interface but has not essentially altered the nature of the application suite. Because these vendors operate on a license fee model to recoup investment in developed technology, very few of these vendors are interested in the development of custom applications, particularly if they do not see an opportunity to resell it. Thus, the sales force automation industry remains focused on productivity at a time when its customers need broad field capabilities to remain competitively relevant. Chapter 2 will address the changes occurring in the marketplace as a whole, and Chapter 6 will outline the implications within the sales automation industry.

A Strategic Perspective

From a technology standpoint, the evolution to open systems, object-oriented programming, powerful design tools, and the emergence of "middleware" creates an environment where organizations can essentially select "best-of-breed" applications and integrate them into a seamless interface. In addition, these same systems tools can be used to develop customized applications that address specific sales and training needs for the organization. This is an exciting era for the end-user community but one that will have major implications for the industry. Although basic applications will remain a necessary ingredient, systems integration will be the vehicle for assembling the sales force automation engine and will be an essential element for the future.

For senior management, these new capabilities offer the ability to more effectively integrate field processes with internal customer fulfillment processes. The result should be highly responsive and performance-laden capabilities for the organization as a whole. A strategic perspective is required to examine the issues of competitiveness and change in the marketplace and convert them into a plan that leverages technology as an enabler. Productivity must be subordinate to competitive advantage and the delivery of superior value to the customer.

There has never been a time when suppliers needed to be closer to their customers. With the rapid course of change in most markets and the intense pressure on margins, survival is going to depend upon having an effective linkage with customers and understanding their needs and priorities. While significant changes hit industry after industry, the most effective mechanism to remain on top is to provide superior sales presence with an organization that is truly "customer driven."

The salesperson must change from a program implementor to a resource that customers can rely on to assist in their drive to remain competitive. For the sales automation industry, this implies providing tools that help to target the right customers and help the salesperson deliver value added to the customer. It also means expanding the linkage between field sales and other functions in a manner that facilitates superior service. If implemented correctly, sales force automation can provide applications which will produce an impact that will be readily apparent to the customer and result in higher margins and volume. Lack of these capabilities will place an organization at a competitive disadvantage and relegate it to lower margin business.

Consistent with this strategic perspective, the next three chapters will develop a strategic model for the sales function that will provide a framework for defining the business needs. The book will then develop these concepts into a road map for implementing a sales automation system.

Endnotes

1.   Peter Drucker, *Management: Tasks, Responsibilities, and Practices* (New York: Harper & Row, 1973), 61.

2.   Roland T. Moriarity and Gordon S. Swartz, "Automation to Boost Sales and Marketing," *Harvard Business Review,* January-February 1989, 100–108.

CHAPTER 2

THE CHANGING COMPETITIVE LANDSCAPE

Concept Formation

This chapter forms a preamble for concepts that follow. The orientation of this book is that sales automation represents a set of tools that, when properly configured and supported, will provide a powerful weapon in a company's overall competitive strategy. To effectively tap into the capability of the technology, the system must be driven by competitive strategy.

Given this context as a foundation, the next step is to discuss the competitive market environment, including trends in procurement. Rather than rely on personal speculation, this chapter contains the insights and perspectives of many experts in this field. Each has a somewhat different emphasis, but the net result of their projections is that suppliers must get closer to their customers and that customers are looking for ways to strengthen their competitive position.

Sales force automation is then discussed in the context of other strategic initiatives that are intended to strengthen competitiveness, such as TQM and reengineering. This may appear to be a digression, but these initiatives have checkered success rates; like sales force automation, they purport to have a customer focus, and they are intended to set the organization apart competitively. There is a pattern to be observed here. As will often be noted, the customer is addressed by backing into rather than starting with him. The fault does not lie with the techniques or the tools but rather with the organizations that are applying them. Sales automation is no exception; it consists of tools and, to a limited extent, a philosophy, but it must be integrated into the whole of how business is conducted.

As indicated throughout this chapter, the future offers a mind-boggling array of market pressures and shifts in economics; having a highly effective system in the hands of the sales organization can mean the difference between flourishing and floundering.

Competition in the 90s and Beyond 2000

The following comments represent the diverse opinions of professionals that specialize in the area of strategic planning:

- While the 50s and 60s were sales oriented and the 70s and 80s were marketing oriented, these emphases are now fading as we enter the customer era.[1] This era is characterized by

  1. seeing customers as valuable assets,

  2. involving current customers as partners,

  3. instituting customer panels to meet with various functional panels,

  4. developing complaint analysis and customer satisfaction surveys, and

  5. involving suppliers in the decision-making process.

- The American Marketing Association labeled the 90s as the "Value Decade."[2] Competitive advantage during this era will be based on the concept of "Total Customer Value," which represents a state in which the quality of a total experience, as perceived by the customer, exceeds its cost.[3]

- "Competition is now a 'war of movement' in which success depends on anticipation of market trends and quick response to changing customer needs."[4]

■ "The only sustainable competitive advantage comes from out-innovating the competition."[5]

■ In one survey of 1,450 executives in 12 global companies, nearly 60% said their competitive environment was in the midst of transformation, and 15% said they should be transforming but had not faced up to change.[6]

■ In a study sponsored by the Gemini Organization, managers rated being organized around customer requirements and being flexible in meeting market conditions as the top 2 of 34 capabilities. According to Francis Gouillart, senior vice president at Gemini, "The past 10 years have shown that protection (due to economies of scale) does not exist. Those barriers have eroded over time."[7]

■ A study of Fortune 1000 companies, conducted by the National Association of Purchasing Management, revealed the following trends (listed in rank order, highest rank first) that will influence purchasing decisions in the future:[8]

1. Fewer sources of supply

2. Customer satisfaction

3. Purchasers managing supplier relations

4. Purchasers aiming at shorter cycle times

5. Supply chain management receiving greater emphasis

6. Engineers and buyers working together as a team

7. Purchasers buying more from foreign producers

8. Ordering more decentralized

9. Teams choosing suppliers

10. Single sourcing increases

■ In a study conducted by Dick Berry at the University of Wisconsin, marketing managers, customer service managers, product managers, and senior executives were asked to define the marketing mix variables they thought were most important but also to rank these in order of importance. The resulting list is could be interpreted as a hierarchy for the 90s:[9]

Item	Rank
Customer sensitivity	1
Product: quality, features, and reliability	2
Customer convenience: availability, easy to do business with	3
Service: pre- and post-sale	4
Price: price charged, terms	5
Place: accessibility, availability	6
Promotion: advertising, publicity, selling	7

■ Daniel Burris, futurist and author of *Technotrends,* projects the following shifts in manufacturing:[10]

From:	To:
Sell what they make	Make what sells
Pre-mfg. to anticipate sales	Mfg. when ordered
Pre-demand mfg.	On-demand mfg.
Mass production	Lean mfg.
Large inventory	JIT
Long cycle times	Short cycle times

■ In their book *Customer Centered Reengineering,* Edwin Crego, Jr. and Peter Schffrin project a similar shift in strategy. Their conclusion is that corporations need to make a transformation from an inward focus to a customer focus as outlined below:[11]

Company-Centered Perspective	Customer-Centered Perspective
■ Organizational hierarchy	■ Customer value hierarchy
■ Products/services	■ Customer value packaging
■ Mass production	■ Customization
■ Durable goods	■ Enduring relationships
■ Zero defects	■ Zero defections

Implications for the Sales Function

Sales executives in the leading sales organizations say that the critical skill salespeople need to develop to achieve long-term customer relationships is *consultative selling*. Strategic need spells the end to the one-size-fits-all solution. In the past, the product was the solution; now, the salesperson must create the solution from a mix of products and services. The better a salesperson is at creatively marshaling all available resources to address a customer's strategic need, the stronger the customer relationship becomes. Customers want salespeople who:

■ Are committed to helping their customers succeed

■ Stay involved with the customer

■ Always focus on the customer's strategic needs

Research conducted by Learning International shows that effective salespeople consistently fulfill three roles:[12]

■ **Strategic Orchestration**

❖ Knowledge of their own company's structure

❖ Expertise in building and managing a team

❖ Ability to manage priorities and performance

❖ Ability to coordinate delivery and service to their customers

❖ Efficiency

❖ Flexibility

■ **Business Consultant**

■ **Long-Term Ally**

Salespeople have to earn the right to be seen as consultative sales-people. Customers say that sales organizations should give salespeople the authority to make important decisions independently. Salespeople should be able to provide creative solutions to strategic problems in an efficient and effective manner. Customers demand more information, ideas, and resources from sales organizations so they can address these needs and achieve their goals.

These observations are consistent with the trends projected for the marketplace and must be supported by the sales automation industry. The capabilities cited above relate to empowerment and the ability to rally the organization around one's sales strategy. Thus, productivity is gained though effectively building programs and partnerships with cus-tomers rather than simply closing new business. The system must help the salesperson to close the business and then expand on that base. The two concepts are intertwined because the customer is interested in what occurs beyond the sale.

Other Strategic Initiatives

The past fifteen years have generated a series of highly publicized techniques and programs that have offered promise of competitive ad-vantage and higher earnings and have, in turn, generated an equally vocal debate regarding their respective merits. Among this list one would have to include **Just In Time (JIT), Total Quality Management (TQM), downsizing or rightsizing, sales force automation**, and **reengineering**. Certainly, the literature supports sterling examples where these techniques have generated extraordinary results and perhaps "saved" companies from competitive extinction; yet on the flip side, there is a mountain of statistics that point to flaws in their application. It is beyond the scope of this book to investigate the various views regarding each of these approaches; however, there are key lessons and similarities that informed professionals need to recognize so that the application of sales automation can benefit from these experiences.

First, it is important that these techniques be perceived correctly; if this is not done, it is easy to confuse the results with the methodology:

- **Just In Time (JIT)** is really a management philosophy that is geared toward elimination of waste. Most of the literature stresses the reduction of inventories, but this is a result of eliminating the factors that generate a need for inventory.

- **Total Quality Management (TQM)** has several definitions, but it also is a management philosophy that dedicates the company to delivery of quality to the customer and continuous improvement initiatives. Similar to JIT, TQM typically uses a number of tools and techniques to support the implementation of the philosophy within the organization.

- **Downsizing** is a management strategy that is designed to flatten organizations, with the intent of reducing costs and improving organizational response time.

- **Reengineering** is a technique that recognizes the need to approach operational improvement from a process perspective. What separates reengineering from other techniques is the emphasis on addressing business processes as an entity, as opposed to breaking the process down into functional segments. The other unique feature of reengineering is the "blank page" approach and the charter to seek radical improvement, which translates into challenging the necessity of each facet of the process, including the need for the process in the first place.

- **Sales Force Automation** consists of a set of networked applications that facilitate the interface between the sales force and the corporation in the support of the customer. It represents an organizational tool.

Strategic Impact

The relationship among all of the above techniques and methodologies is that they all represent tools that have the potential to help organizations improve their operational performance and perhaps (one does not guarantee the other) their competitive position. As indicated earlier, each of these approaches has a checkered history in terms of success rate. This is to be expected, because each approach must be understood in the context of organizational strategy and intent. They are not self-fulfilling. Management context and competency are critical, as indicated in the following statistics and observations:

Total Quality Management

■ In a survey conducted by MAPI (Manufacturers' Alliance for Productivity and Innovation), major organizations using TQM were asked to evaluate their results.[13] The following was reported:

   ❖ 40% significant improvement

   ❖ 45% some improvement

   ❖ 15% marginal improvement

   ❖ 0% no improvement

■ In a survey conducted by Arthur D. Little, 36% of executives from U.S. corporations believed that their quality process improved their competitiveness.

■ A survey of senior mangers at 95 U.S. companies, conducted by Rath and Strong, reported that 38% gave their quality programs failing marks.

Downsizing

■ In their book *Customer Centered Reengineering*, Edwin Crego, Jr. and Peter Schiffrin identify some statistics that give cause for reflection.[14] Based on a study of 100 companies that have downsized:

❖ Only 19% reported an increase in competitive advantage.

❖ 90% hoped to reduce expenses; less than 50% did.

❖ 75% hoped for productivity improvement; only 22% achieved this.

❖ 50% expected to reduce bureaucracy and speed decisions; only 15% did.

■ A study by Mercer Management Consulting in Lexington, MA, suggests that the downsizing spree of recent years has left companies leaner but not richer. The survey of 180 U.S. executives indicated that growth is a top priority.[15] The quest for organizational effectiveness through downsizing, reengineering, and productivity management continues to be of top concern to senior management.

Reengineering

■ Even the advocates of reengineering point out that 50–70% of organizations that undertake reengineering efforts do not achieve the dramatic results they intended (James Champy).

Sales Force Automation

■ Both the Gartner Group and Culpepper and Associates have positioned the failure rate of sales force automation as greater than 60%.

The first conclusion one must reach is that no initiative or technique is a ticket to competitive stardom. Obviously, some organizations have been successful while others have not garnered that same level of improvement. Given the rate of change within the marketplace and the enormous costs associated with pursuing any of these initiatives, there is a profound need to be successful. One senses that there is a window of opportunity within the marketplace and that once closed, it will be very difficult to recover anywhere near the current competitive position. With this perspective in mind, it is doubly important to learn from the experience of others and map out a strategy that provides a reasonable balance of risk vs. quantum improvement. The following observations by experts in their respective fields provide valuable insight regarding how to set up an environment for success.

■ In a study of senior quality executives at 78 Fortune 500 companies:

  ❖ Roughly 33% reported substantial positive impact on performance (revenue, market share, and profit margin).

  ❖ The other 67% reported no market impact.

■ Overall, when asked about specifics of their programs, the respondents indicated the following:

  ❖ Only 51% said they had active executive involvement.

  ❖ Only 40% said they used customer research to form their quality strategy.

  ❖ Only 34% said they used customer research for guiding change efforts.

■ Interestingly, 85% of the successful firms had all three, while only 10% of those who said their program had no effect had all three; therefore, one could consider the following as critical success factors:

  ❖ Executive involvement and leadership throughout the process.

  ❖ A strategic customer-centered orientation with on-going customer satisfaction measurement.

  ❖ A change program strategy for improvement that is integrated and linked to the business's purpose and processes.

■ According to a report by Pittiglio and McGrath, there are a variety of reasons why companies fail at implementing TQM:[16]

  ❖ A management team that is resistant to change.

  ❖ TQM education carried out without linkage to specific change activities.

❖ A lack of clear practical objectives within a company's corporate culture.

■ James Harrington with Ernst and Young reports the following primary reasons why improvement efforts fail:

❖ Upper management does not believe that they have to change.

❖ Lack of trust between management and employees.

❖ Wrong person selected as the "improvement champion" for the wrong reasons.

❖ Limited capabilities of the consultant.[17]

■ Mobilization begins at the top with a vision and a business idea, but the energy comes from pushing authority and accountability down to where the action is. The CEO cannot do it all. There must be a critical mass of people in the company at both upper and middle levels who are really committed to make change happen.

■ "Inevitably, in even the best of such companies, workers are never really judged by the standards of utility to the customer. Instead, they're judged by how well they work for the supposed bosses of the hierarchy from the CEO on down. In other words, performance measurement is entirely a function of internal requirements, either bureaucratic, political, or personal."[18]

■ "The dominant improvement techniques of the past decade or more—downsizing, cost cutting, productivity improvement, total quality management, and reengineering have been almost entirely internally or company focused. This myopia eventually leads to blindness."[19]

■ Why TQM fails:[20]

❖ Failure of upper management to be personally involved in their company's efforts toward quality.

❖ Mounted as a stand-alone program, unconnected to marketing strategies, rigidly and narrowly applied and expected to produce a miraculous transformation.

❖ Often not customer focused but rather internal programs run by technocrats.

❖ Company attempts to do too much too quickly.

■ Why reengineering fails:

❖ Tactical vs. strategic application. When reengineering is deployed tactically, its focus and scope tend to be limited to a single process or within a function. It targets work flow almost exclusively to reduce costs, head count, and required office space.

❖ When deployed strategically, focus is on critical core processes. The team takes a holistic view of organizational change, targeting systems, organizational structure, incentives and corporate culture, in addition to work flow.

Basic Learning

Senior Management Involvement and Commitment

A common theme within these observations is that senior management must be convinced of the need to change. These programs cannot be successfully implemented as a bottom-up initiative. The reasons for this are clear: the initiatives require significant resources, and they must be tied concretely to the strategic direction of the company.

O.D. Resources, a change management constancy based in Atlanta, GA, equates willingness to change with "pain management." Pain can either represent a current or future state. Thus, management's willingness to change is directly related to their inference of consequences relative to the status quo vs. the implications of implementing relevant initiatives. If this model is accurate, then management will take the appropriate action and stay the course if they perceive the pain of action to be less than the pain of inaction.

Clarity and Constancy of Purpose

Given this model, it is equally obvious that without well-articulated goals which are tied to the strategic direction of the company, senior management commitment is likely to wane. An associated risk is that the initiative will drift and lose its focus, resulting in a lack of desired results and a waste of resources.

Objectives That Are Customer Centered

Goals that are based on internal criteria are likely to be linked to organizational or political needs. The result is that the initiative does not leverage the competitive position of the organization. When competitors start grabbing market share through improved services or performance, the only option is to reduce price, which will quickly erode any cost savings represented by the initiative.

Changing the Culture

Changing the culture is relevant only to the extent that the organization pursues a strategy of better serving the customer. The reason for this is that customer-oriented strategies offer the potential to lead the market and garner higher profitability. Failure to do this implies lost share, diminishing profitability, and mediocrity. Thus, the framework can be set for managing pain (change) throughout the organization. A customer focus is the most viable way of rallying the organization and removing the context of internal politics that will blunt, if not subvert, the initiative.

Business-Related Cycles in the 21st Century

Global competition, the speed of change, and the need for customer focus represent new and perhaps unprecedented pressures on companies in the current decade and beyond. The purpose of this section will be to describe these demands in sufficient detail so that the relevance for sales force automation can be introduced later in this context.

Three cyclical processes will be discussed in this section. In the future, it is expected that these cycles will shorten in length or be more pronounced in effect; how a company responds to them may well determine the viability of the firm. The cycles include:

■ Business cycles

■ Product life cycles

■ Business design cycles

In each case, customer interface and corporate strategy will be outlined to define the opportunity for improved sales performance.

Business Cycles

Business cycles pertain to the rise and fall of national output. In the past, international companies could, at least in part, depend on export to assist in adverse economic times. Increasingly, the market is becoming a world market, thereby accentuating economic conditions. From a corporate perspective, the national economic picture can have dire implications (commodity chemical) or the business may be relatively unaffected (food processing). For companies which operate in industries that are strongly impacted by swings in the economy, a logical strategy is to establish and maintain a mix of customers with the following attributes:

■ Balance demand across business cycles.

■ Are able to pass through cost increases when demand is tight.

■ Serve industries that are less volatile to swings in the economy.

■ Operate in a counter-cyclical pattern than the economy as a whole.

According to this scenario, the sales function must work closely with marketing in the search for the best customer mix. Segmentation of the market will certainly reflect criteria outside the mainstream of practices, such as sensitivity to economic conditions and end markets served (demand behavior and ability to pass through price increases). This represents an entirely different customer-acquisition process.

Product Life Cycle

The classical product life cycle curve can be described as portrayed in Figure 2.1. The vertical axis represents revenue per annum, while the horizontal axis represents time. The product curve consists of four phases:

1. *Introductory period* where awareness and availability of the product are established.

2. *Growth period* where the product gains acceptance and serves pent up demand.

3. *Maturity period* where substitute products become available and the market becomes saturated relative to the product's potential.

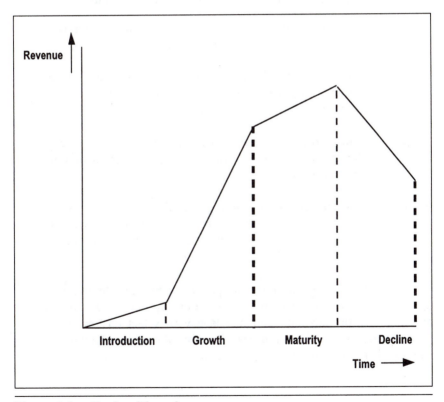

Figure 2.1   Product life cycle curve.

4. *Decline period* where demand declines or superior choices are available in the market.

Across most industries, the product life cycle is being compressed. From a sales function perspective, this means that market penetration must occur at a faster rate. Failure to achieve rapid penetration will strongly impact market share and, more importantly, profitability.

Obviously, if product life cycles are shortened, then product development time must be reduced. Many product development methodologies and technologies have been developed to facilitate the duration of this process. However, the real driver for the methodology must be a solid understanding of the industry and customer needs. Guiding the organization to the sources of influence and movers and shakers of the industry should be a key role of the sales organization. To operate in this capacity, the sales force must have the following capabilities:

1. The sales force must understand its role and have established criteria for these opinion leaders, etc.

2. The sales force must be supported in its effort to gain access (sell) to these organizations (i.e., there must be alignment of purpose within the organization).

3. The sales force must be able to build trust and a partnership relationship to effectively gain access to the right people in the organization.

4. Beyond the specifics of the high-profile accounts, the sales organization must be able to provide input to the organization relative to competitive moves and the priorities of other aspects of the market.

Thus, the sales organization can provide a crucial role in developing the right interfaces so that the product development and strategic elements of the organization can interface with select customers to best utilize limited time and resources. The objective is to effectively anticipate needs before others recognize them.

Business Design Cycles

Adrian Slywotzky, partner with Computer Decisions, Inc., defines a business design as the entire system for delivering utility to customers and earning a profit from that activity.[21] The business design includes:

■ Selection of customers

■ Differentiation strategy

■ Determination of tasks to be outsourced

■ Resource configuration

■ Approach to the market

■ Creation of value for customers

■ Positioning to capture maximum profit

The key concept is that companies make these decisions based on assumptions regarding the market and how to best maximize profitability within the structure of the market. Once established, corporations tend to operate on these assumptions without periodically reviewing them for relevance. Developments over the past decade have demonstrated that business design exhibits the same characteristics as product cycles. The duration of the cycle is likely to be longer than a product cycle, but in the turbulent global economic times of the future, it is likely that this cycle will also become compressed. The implications of the business design are that having the best product does not automatically result in superior market position or the highest profitability. For example, Dell Computers changed the basis for delivering high-quality customized personal computers, garnered a major portion of the market, and, more importantly, captured more of the profit potential of the market. Another notable example of this phenomenon is Microsoft. In addition, one can't overlook the implications of the Internet to change the balance of power and profitability in the market. Some other examples of business design are provided in the next table:

Business Design	United Airlines	Southwest Airlines
Key Elements:	Hub and spoke High fixed costs Dominate hub	Point to point Low, flexible cost Dominate route
Key Assumptions:	Scale reduces cost	City-pair demand sufficient to be profitable

Business Design	Traditional Auto	Toyota
Key Elements:	Product focus Rigid mfg. system Backward integration	Customer focus Flexible mfg. Specialization
Key Assumptions:	Technology and scale drive success One way to do business	Customer under- standing drives success Innovative improve- ment processes

In each of the comparative situations presented above, it is apparent how key assumptions can lead to different operating philosophies and performance. The important point to carry away from this section is that business design assumptions need to be approached as a cyclical process. If the organization does not renew its assumptions and actively anticipate the best competitive positioning for profit capture, **someone else will determine its future**. The relevance from a sales function perspective is that the organization must consistently ask itself:

■ How are customers changing?

■ What are customer priorities?

■ What are the profit drivers within the industry?

Certainly the first two questions need to be driven by the sales function. The challenge is to approach the topic in a way that maximizes corporate value and ultimately aids the sales organization.

Competitive Advantage: Staying Close to the Customer

Joseph Pine II, in his pioneering book *Mass Customization*, outlines a list of trends and techniques which he felt would dominate the competitive landscape of the 90s. These items included:[22]

Time-based competition	Proliferating variety	JIT production
Regional marketing	Continual improvements	Shortened product life cycles
Market-driven quality	Globalization	Networked organizations
Micro-marketing	Increased customization	Lean production
Cycle time reduction	TQM	Flattened hierarchy
Computer-integrated mfg.	Process reengineering	Heightened importance of service
Quick responses	Flexible mfg. systems	Database marketing

Few people would argue that the items in this table are not relevant. What tends to be confusing is how these items tie together. The answer is found in the business design concept presented in the previous section. In previous eras, the business design issue rarely occurred or happened at a rate that was easier to react to. In today's market, a shift in business design can occur from a company that is not even a current competitor and at a rate that denies reasonable response time. In this context, these items are tools or facets of the larger issue. Competitiveness in today's market and into the future is driven by the customer, and the challenge is to construct the most effective business design to meet these needs. Thus, it is likely that business designs will need to change at unprecedented levels, which is a parallel concept to those who are advocating organizational renewal. Gary Hamel and C. K. Prahalad position this concept in terms of foresight vs. vision. "Industry foresight is based on deep insights into the trends in technology, demographics, regulations, and lifestyles that can be harnessed to rewrite industry rules and create new competitive space."[23]

In order to maintain correct insight and knowledge of the industry, one has to be close to the customer. In order to better understand or appreciate methods for improving this insight, it is valuable to know what gets in the way of creating this perspective. The American Quality Foundation and Ernst and Young conducted a research study regarding organizations whose strategic documents relegated customer service to a secondary level of importance.[24] The study revealed four basic impediments common among these organizations:

- Executive wrong-headedness (satisfy the boss rather than the customer)

- Silo management (functional structure and performance measures)

- Hardened arteries (organization memory dictates future)

- Policies and procedure represent an organizational straight-jacket

On the other side of the spectrum, The GAO reviewed the performance of twenty companies that scored the highest on the Baldrige examination during 1988–90. They found six TQM-related elements that contribute to improved performance:[25]

- Focus on meeting customer quality requirements

- Top management leadership in disseminating TQM values

- Employee empowerment through continuous improvement

- A flexible and responsive corporate culture

- A fact-based decision-making system

- Partnerships with suppliers used to improve product and service quality

These findings are virtually a polar opposite to the impediments of the organizations that gave customer service a secondary priority.

Given the complexity of the market, the challenges of organizational change, and the checkered success rates of current improvement processes, there are two clear points:

■ Success will be determined by delivering superior value to the customer.

■ Success will be determined by capturing maximum profit in the delivery of that value.

The question then is where to start. Although TQM and reengineering advocate a customer focus, in practice, these techniques often are applied to processes that are not directly connected with the customer. The model presented in Chapter 3 starts with the customer and identifies the processes that touch the customer and then works backward from that point. The rationale for this approach is as follows:

■ If customer value is an objective, then the starting place must address what is delivered currently and how the customer perceives its utility.

■ By starting with processes that directly touch the customer, then improvements will be immediately apparent to the customer.

■ Working directly back from the customer is more likely to maintain the customer's perspective, and performance measures are more likely to reflect true value added.

■ The results should occur faster because the changes will be felt in the marketplace.

By definition, this approach directly confronts the sales process and the alignment of sales and the corporation in the delivery of value to the customer. This perspective also provides an effective framework for defining systems needs of the field organization.

Endnotes

1. Earl Naumann and Patrick Shannon, *Business Horizons*, November-December 1992, 44–52.

2. Edwin T. Crego, Jr. and Peter D. Schiffrin, *Customer Centered Reengineering* (New York: Irwin, 1995), 22.

3. Ibid.

4. George Stalk and Philip Evans, "Time Based Competition," *Harvard Business Review*, March-April 1992, 62.

5. James F. Morse, "Predators and Prey: A New Ecology of Competition," *Harvard Business Review*, May-June 1993, 75.

6. Eileen Davis, "What's on American Managers' Minds?" *Management Review*, April 1995, 15.

7. Ibid.

8. Barry Retchfeld, *Personal Selling Power*, September 1993, 26–33.

9. D. Berry, *Marketing News*, December 24, 1990, 10.

10. Roger Burris, *Technotrends* (New York: Harper Business, 1993), 350.

11. Crego and Schiffrin, *Customer Centered Reengineering*, 20.

12. Kevin J. Corcoran et al., *High Performance Sales Organizations* (Chicago: Irwin, 1995), 51.

13. H. James Harrington, *Total Improvement Management* (New York: McGraw-Hill, 1995), 28.

14. Crego and Schiffrin, *Customer Centered Reengineering*, 9.

15. Ibid., 18.

16. Rabin Pittiglio and Todd McGrath, "Why Companies Fail at TQM," *IIE Solutions*, May 1995, 14.

17. Harrington, *Total Improvement Management*, 44–47.

18. James Champy, *Reengineering Management* (New York: Harper Business, 1995), 124.

19. Crego and Schiffrin, *Customer Centered Reengineering*, 181.

20. William C. Johnson and Richard J. Chvala, *Total Quality in Marketing* (Delray Beach, FL: St. Lucie Press, 1996), 12–13.

21. Adrian J. Slywotzky, *Value Migration* (Boston: Harvard Business School Press, 1995), 25–27.

22. B. Joseph Pine II, *Mass Customization* (Boston: Harvard Business School Press, 1993), 34.

23. Gary Hamel and C. K. Prahalad, *Competing for the Future* (Boston: Harvard Business School Press, 1994), 76.

24. Harrington, 148.

25. Brian Usilaner and Michael Dulworthy, "What's the Bottom Line Payback for TQM?" *Journal for Quality and Participation*, March 1992, 82–90.

CHAPTER 3

ORGANIZATIONAL MODELS AND ASSUMPTIONS

Stovepipe Structure

Although there have been various experiments with organizational structure over the past thirty years, the hierarchical, functional model remains the model most often encountered in industry today. Figure 3.1 provides a representation of this model. This model will be used throughout the chapter.

Functional organization groupings are often referred to as silos or stovepipes of power. Certainly they have that graphical appearance, but in many organizations, the power flows vertically within these structures, and cross-functional planning and coordination occur along strict guidelines or not at all. Even when downsizing occurs, the basic structure does not change, and layers are simply removed, as reflected in Figure 3.2.

What is important to note regarding these structures are the implicit assumptions regarding their form.

1. Functional structure contributes to efficiency of the operation through economies of scale.

2. The output of each function is the entity to optimize.

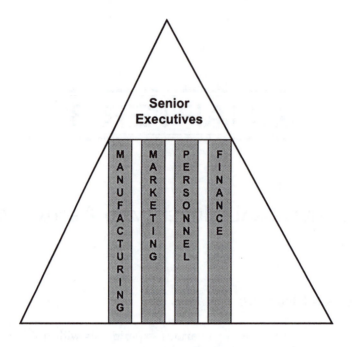

Figure 3.1   Typical hierarchical organizational structure.

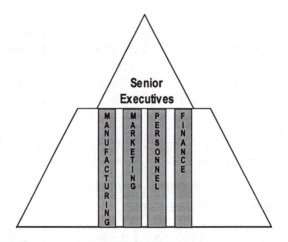

Figure 3.2   Effect of downsizing on a hierarchical structure.

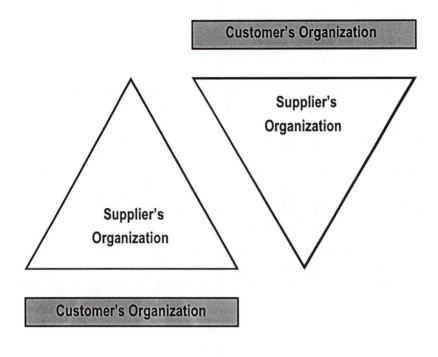

Figure 3.3   Hierarchical organizational structure with concept of the customer being the driver of the organization.

Chapter 2 outlined forces and trends in the marketplace that will form the basis for competitive advantage in the future. The majority of the themes centered on the customer and the need for responsiveness in virtually all aspects of market performance. Recognizing these needs, some strategists have inverted the pyramid, thereby indicating the customer needs to be on top.

Although the motives for positioning the customer above the organizational structure are well intended, the concept sends two very erroneous and perhaps dangerous signals:

1.   In each of the configurations in Figure 3.3, senior executives are the furthest removed from the customer. Although that may be true in practice, it is not something to memorialize in a diagram, and it is certainly a strategic and operational error.

2. Upside down or right side up, this model creates the illusion that the customer is, in fact, served directly by the functional groups in a vertical process.

The error of these schematics could be overlooked if it were not for the fact that many organizations do their planning and goal setting with this precise model in mind. It is not uncommon to see annual and 5-year plans created within each silo and the collective plans only meet at the top, where they become so aggregated that the incongruity is hard to see. The reality is that most operational processes are horizontal in nature. TQM practitioners approach this dilemma with cross-functional teams, while reengineering establishes a member of senior management to serve as a "process owner." This cross-functional flow is depicted in Figure 3.4.

Even when the cross-functional nature of processes is accounted for in the analysis, there is still the hurdle of what metrics to apply to assess improvement or the scope of improvement. One of the blind spots of both

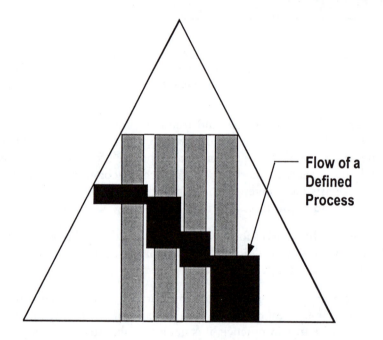

Flow of a Defined Process

Figure 3.4   Cross-functional nature of operational processes.

Figure 3.5   Thinking "Inside the Box."

TQM and reengineering is that improvement criteria may take on an internal focus. Consider what happens when a reengineering project identifies a major opportunity for cost improvement but has major structural implications. What is the driving force? Everyone recognizes the need to be efficient and maintain costs, but organizational pain must be balanced against the pain of not acting, and this is where the rock and hard spot exist. When opportunities are driven by strictly internal criteria, it takes exceptional executive courage to act upon them. Perhaps this is a contributing factor to the low success rate of actual reengineering breakthroughs. No matter how well the technique is applied, if an internal "four wall" mind-set (Figure 3.5) is used, the analysis starts out in a box and will stay in the limitations of the box.

Thinking **outside the box** really implies utilizing **an external perspective**. In this regard, the next section will outline an approach for capturing this external perspective.

A Holistic Customer-Based Model

A "holistic model" implies a view or perspective that embraces the total process associated with the item being modeled. As the title implies, this section will introduce a model that reflects the realities in the marketplace as experienced by the customer. This view is consistent with both TQM and reengineering techniques; however, in practice, these techniques are often not explicitly driven from the customer perspective, or the approach may be trivialized to the point of essentially being four-wall thinking.

The model will utilize the hierarchical organizational structure introduced earlier in this chapter. The point of departure from the original model is that it will focus on supplier performance from the customer's perspective. The emphasis will be on the "moments of truth" where product, service, or contact directly impacts the customer. These moments of truth form the basis of reality for the customer. All of the supplier's efforts in terms of image, advertising, collateral, productivity, and systems dissolve into what the customer actually experiences.

Never before has this perspective been more appropriate. With the evolution of sophisticated procurement systems and total quality programs, customers are increasingly approaching a total system context for evaluating vendors. The customer often knows more about the performance of a product/service than the supplier does. In the past, it may have been possible to employ pricing or influence strategies to counter weaknesses in delivery against the moments of truth, but these strategies are going to evolve into lower market share and profitability.

The foundation for the model is to recognize that the moments of truth that the customer experiences are the result of cross-functional processes; thus, the holistic customer-based model takes the form shown in Figure 3.6.

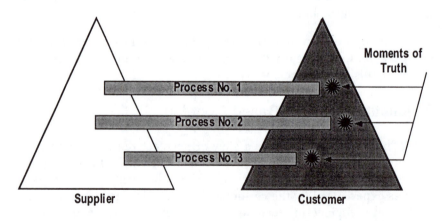

Figure 3.6   Cross-functional processes and moments of truth.

Each one of the bars joining the organizations represents a process. Examples of these processes could include:

1. Quotes and pricing

2. Order fulfillment

3. Product customization

4. Packaging customization

5. Delivery logistics

6. Post-delivery installation

7. Warranty

8. Invoicing

9. Service/maintenance

10. Training

11. Returns/customer complaints

Virtually every process is a composite effort of more than one function. Thus, the focus is on the moment of truth. Understandably, how the customer views these moments of truth is valuable, but still more valuable is how these moments of truth hold up against the needs and priorities of the organization. Further, what type or level of performance would clearly differentiate the supplier?

Recognizing that business-to-business transactions involve a customer who is competing in an end market, the question becomes even broader. How do the moments of truth contribute to the customer's competitive capability? This relationship is reflected in Figure 3.7.

In this context, the supplier would seek to define how the customer competes in the marketplace and how the processes can be leveraged to increase value to the customer and thereby improve margins for the supplier. This takes the analysis out of the "four-wall" context and into the

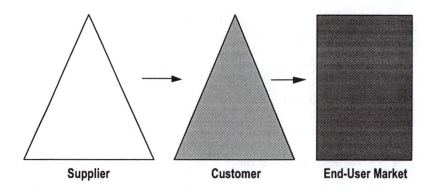

Figure 3.7   Supplier, customer, and end-market configuration.

larger world of competitiveness where motivational and directional tools, such as vision and mission, can truly tap into the strength of the organization. The voice of the customer is truly being sought in a construct that can be utilized within the supplier's organization.

To demonstrate how this approach might be applied, consider the processes outlined earlier:

1. Quotes and Pricing

- Quote turnover time can be critical to organizations that are trying to reduce their cycle times.

- Quote accuracy can save wasted administrative time for both suppliers and customers. Quote accuracy has at least two dimensions: (1) specify the right solution and (2) provide a complete quote.

- Accessibility can be an issue if there are time zones involved or the customer works around the clock on a 7-day work schedule.

- Pricing application must be clear, and where appropriate, pricing may be in the form of a formula that helps customers better plan their own costs and pricing.

- Payment terms may represent a major value to a customer. This is particularly true when working capital is a major concern of the organization. Programs that allow customers to take ownership of items when they are actually used in the process can offer considerable cash-flow relief.

2. Order Fulfillment

- Cycle time can be a major concern. The ability to support JIT commitments or otherwise provide short turnaround time can impact working capital and flexibility of response for the customer.

- An allied characteristic is the speed with which the supplier can commit to a delivery date. This reduces cycle time and administrative costs for the customer.

- Accessibility of the order fulfillment system by the customer can be critical if there are time zones involved or if the customer is operating on a 24-hour, 7-day-a-week basis.

- Accuracy is a key criteria; delivery of the wrong item adds value to no one.

- The cost efficiency of the order fulfillment process can be another factor. Use of EDI and/or JIT electronic interfaces can reduce transaction costs while reducing inventories and overall cycle time.

3. Product Design/Customization

- Rapid turnaround on these processes is essential to customers who are working to reduce their cycle times.

- For flat organizations, simplicity of coordination and reliability are a must to keep administrative costs down.

- The customer would certainly be interested in the manufacturability of the supplier's item and how it adds to or detracts from the operational environment.

- Customers may be interested in operating on a partnership basis with a supplier if they provide requisite expertise that the customer does not want to retain in-house.

4. Delivery Logistics

■ Both flexible manufacturing and JIT processes demand delivery times that are defined to the hour. The advantage to the customer is reduced floor space, reduced inventory, reduced handling, and, sometimes, reduction in damage and rework.

5. Post-Delivery Installation

■ Cycle time reduction is often the key in this type of service. Reduction in installation cycle time can be tied to opportunity costs for the customer.

6. Warranty

■ Application of the warranty should be clear and easy to process by the customer.

■ Cycle time to process warranty claims should be minimized.

■ Warranty processes should feed continuous improvement to enhance reliability, training, and reduce warranty response time.

7. Invoicing

■ Accurate and complete information should be provided and in a format that facilitates the customer's internal process.

■ Invoicing should take on a format and frequency consistent with customer needs. For example, monthly consolidated invoices.

8. Service/Maintenance

■ Response time, failure rates, and maintenance costs are obvious customer concerns.

■ Use of preventive maintenance and actual system monitoring are other ways of ensuring "up-time" and proper productivity of the customer's equipment.

■ Accessibility can be another issue. Can the customer receive help on a 24-hour, 7-day-a-week basis?

9. Training

■ Training can pertain to the design, use, and/or maintenance of a product. The quality of the training could be based on the time required vs. its effectiveness in helping the customer reach internal performance targets.

■ Updates on training via other media such as teleconference, VHS tapes, or interactive computer programs can reduce overall training costs for the customer.

10. Complaints/Returns

■ Complaints and returns should be viewed as a vital insight regarding the expectations of the customer. In this regard, internal processes should make it easy for customers to complain.

■ Cycle time reduction and accessibility are also key considerations.

■ Documentation from these processes should feed continuous improvement processes.

Performance from a Market Perspective

The four-wall mindset would approach these basic processes from the standpoint of reducing costs, reducing internal risk, improving cash flow, and leveraging productivity. Even with tools such as activity-based costing, an internal focus does not tend to consider the concept of value or competitiveness. Therein lies the weakness. Particularly in turbulent market conditions, an internal perspective will "save" the company out of competition.

Getting close to the customer implies understanding the following four characteristics:

1. How customers compete in their respective markets.

2. How customers utilize purchased product/service and its effectiveness in leveraging their level of competitiveness.

3. How customers value various process interfaces.

4. What the priorities of customers are.

Ideally, for each process, the supplier organization should be able to assess improvement from the customer's perspective vs. internal criteria.

The graph in Figure 3.8 represents relationships that cannot always be precisely known in most cases; however, it does reflect the relationships that a supplier would be seeking. In general, one would seek to provide value that can be produced at an efficient price and seek customers who are willing to pay a premium price for that corresponding value. By plotting this type of data, organizations can guard against tendencies to improve processes or products in ways not valued by the customer base.

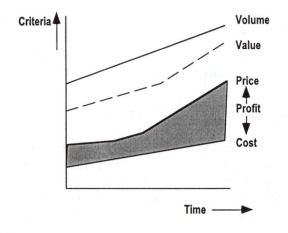

Figure 3.8   Relationship between value, cost, and price.

Expanding the Model to Channel Management

Another feature of Figure 3.8 is that it provides a model for evaluating the effectiveness of channel alternatives. By studying the value needs and

priorities of customer groupings, one can begin to assess the appropriateness of channel alternatives. Each alternative may provide different levels
of cost and price; thus, factoring in competitive risk, one can begin to
rationalize a channel strategy. However, one complication is that if the
channel represents a separate organization, such as a distributor, then
who is the customer? Is it the distributor or the distributor's customer or
the ultimate end user? In reality, it is all of the above. Figure 3.9 provides
a schematic of this more complicated situation.

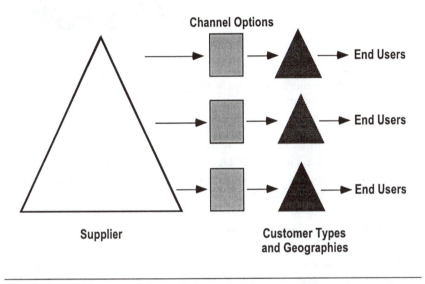

Figure 3.9   Conceptual view of channel options supplying unique customer
groupings and end users.

Thus, the model can deal with a wide variety of businesses including
consumer goods. In expanding the process model to incorporate the
concept of cross-functional processes, the model appears as shown in
Figure 3.10.

The character of the process/value analysis does not change when
channel decisions are introduced. Figure 3.10 represents a number of
processes interfacing with the channel and then being directed to the
supplier or the customer, depending on the respective direction of the
process flow. The complication is that value must be added to the channel

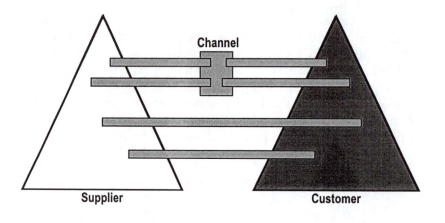

Figure 3.10   Integrating the concept of channel management with the customer-oriented processes.

entity, and the channel entity must add value to the customer. The lower process bars on the chart reflect processes that involve direct linkage between the customer and the supplier. This whole concept will be expanded in the next chapter.

Choosing Your Customers

If markets were homogeneous in terms of needs, value expectations, and price/value sensitivity, each customer would essentially be equally desirable subject to its respective volume potential. The reality of today's market is that it is fractious and fast changing. Customer attitudes toward value pricing, what constitutes value, and the ability to pass through costs to the end user are all relevant issues for choosing who to do business with. Simply stated, a supplier wants to sell to customers who are willing to pay incrementally more for that value which the supplier can most effectively provide.

In any market, there will tend to be a distribution of leadership that follows the classical "bell-shaped" curve as described in Figure 3.11.

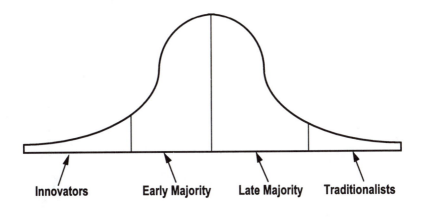

Figure 3.11   Distribution of innovation within a market.

The challenge for any supplier that competes on a value-added basis is to define the ideal customers to do business with. If one wishes to stay ahead of the market, the choice is clear that one would desire to target innovators. The next chapter will discuss the sales process and how to link the targeting of customers with the delivery of value.

CHAPTER 4

THE SALES PROCESS

Chapter 3 developed the concept that processes which touch the customer are essentially horizontal in nature. It was demonstrated that each process is connected with one or more moments of truth that the customer experiences. The collection of these moments of truth forms the image of the supplier and defines the working relationship between the companies. By understanding the characteristics of these moments of truth and how the customer base values these characteristics, a supplier organization has a clear charter for process improvement that will leverage the sales process.

This chapter expands these concepts by presenting a model sales process. The purpose of the model is to provide a clearer picture of the role of sales as an interface with internal functions and as an interface with the customer. At this point, the discussion will describe the rationale for the model; in subsequent chapters, the model will be expanded to discuss integration with the processes and the role of sales force automation in leveraging the overall sales effort.

The Basic Model

Most references to sales process limit their attention to what is essentially a customer acquisition process. Although this is an important facet of selling, the building of customer relationships and the expansion

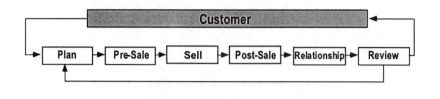

Figure 4.1   Basic sales-process model.

of the business must also be considered as part of the overall process, as Figure 4.1 shows.

Virtually any sales process can be described in the context of the above process steps:

1. **Plan**: Define priorities, the approach to the market, how success is going to be tracked, and what material and resources are going to be required.

2. **Pre-Sale**: This stage of the process includes contacting prospects and targeting sales efforts to maximize results. Learning is an important aspect of this stage; the salesperson gains knowledge regarding the potential of the account while establishing personal and company credibility.

3. **Sell**: The line between Pre-Sale and Sell is gray; however, the process moves toward actual development of quotes or bids. This may be part of the credibility development, but it involves a different set of processes. Therefore, the preparation of sales-related documents will be considered in this phase.

4. **Post-Sale**: This stage embraces all activities that occur after the order is submitted. It includes order follow-up, delivery/installation, and service thereafter.

5. **Relationship Building**: Once a presence has been established, there is a need to protect that relationship and expand upon it. Research studies have indicated that it costs five times more to secure a new customer than it does to get an order from an existing customer.

6. **Review**: There are two facets of review. One is the review of business and status of the business with the account. The other facet is reviewing account performance as input to the planning process for the next planning period; hence, the arrow returning to the Planning step.

Using these basic definitions, each step of the process will be examined from the perspective of the processes involved and the other activities supported within the step.

Planning Phase

The planning phase can be generalized as encompassing the activities and processes outlined in Figure 4.2.

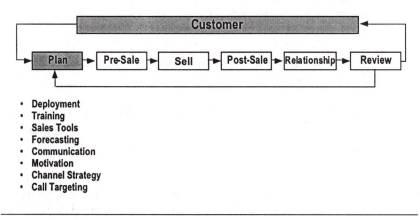

Figure 4.2   Planning phase of the generalized sales process.

Deployment

Deployment covers the task of allocating limited resources to specific geographical, account, and industry designations. For a direct sales force, at the strategic level this decision can have virtually a "make or break" context (IBM, for example). This process can also be related to decisions regarding sales force structure, such as job levels, product responsibilities, and span of control.

At the market level, the sales manager must develop an equally strategic plan to deploy resources on a more micro level, sometimes with more complex issues, such as the chemistry of accounts vs. personality of salespeople, etc.

Training

Training can be segmented by type and content as follows:

- **Competence Training**: This category pertains to providing fundamental instruction regarding the company, policies, the product, the processes, and selling techniques. It represents the minimal knowledge and skill base required to be in the field.

- **On-Going Product Training**: Pertains to the continuous training regarding products and services offered by the company.

- **On-Going Skill Training**: Reinforcement and refinement of selling-related skills.

- **Coaching and Counseling**: Typically, the desired interface between field manager and salesperson when in the field.

Clearly, some of these training-related activities are definitely "plan" related, while others are more spontaneous. For simplicity, it is desirable to catalog them as being in this portion of the sales process.

Sales Tools

Sales tools represents a broad category of resources that are available to the salesperson to educate the customer, specify the product/services, and/or position the product and company. This category would include the following list of items (by no means an exhaustive list):

- Product and company literature

- Samples

- Specification sheets

- Success stories

- Price lists

- Forms (customer related)

- Plant tours

- References

- Account information (syndicated sources)

- Access to technical assistance

- Negotiation tools

For most salespeople, sales tools are directly correlated with what they can carry in the truck of their car.

Forecasting

The scope of this category is intended to include both the development of an annual plan and periodic updates relative to monthly and/or quarterly projections. Annual plan figures often include a projection of both revenue and expenses. Monthly forecasts typically involve 30-, 60-, or 90-day projections.

Communication

As with several of these categories, there are multi-dimensions to the topic. Obviously, day-to-day operations require on-going communication, and that is assumed to be present throughout the sales process. However, there is a strategic or directional level of communication that needs to take place to ensure that the field is "connected" to the status and orientation of the corporation at large.

Motivation

Motivation as implied in the planning phase pertains to the establishment of goals and bonus structures that direct the sales effort in the "right" direction. It may also include recognition capabilities that are formal (dinners, president's council, etc.) or informal (pat on the back or informal note).

Channel Strategy

A channel strategy essentially embodies the rationale for using each element of the channel strategy along with the attendant support structure, pricing, and goals.

Call Targeting

Call targeting suggests that the salesperson either has developed or has been given targets regarding "A, B, C" accounts and relative expected frequency of calls and time commitment. This type of information is typically integrated into the deployment process, but it may be a secondary or continuous refinement in the field.

Pre-Sale

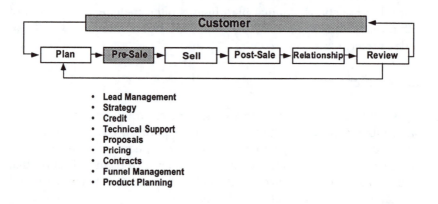

Figure 4.3   Pre-sale activities within the sales process.

Lead Management

Lead management relates to the handling of leads from the processing/qualification standpoint but also from the evaluation of performance perspective.

Account Sales Strategy

An account strategy can have two levels. One level addresses securing a new account, while the other level pertains to expanding business with an existing customer.

Credit

Credit issues typically occur at two points within the sales process: one point is in the pre-sales or first order acceptance phase, while the other is an on-going receivables status issue.

Technical Support

This type of support may take the form of field level engineers or technical expertise, or it may be corporate-based R&D assistance. This assistance may be directed at gaining credibility for the company and/or may be required to specify the product/service during the proposal stage.

Proposals

Proposals covers the entire process of generating specifications, creating samples, and creating proposals and quotations.

Pricing

Pricing is an integral part of generating proposals; however, it is represented as a separate process because price negotiation sometimes follows the submission of a quote. In a broader context, pricing includes the negotiation and approval processes for price deviations.

Contracts

Once the scope of the quote and pricing have been established, there is often a contract process that establishes the final content and signatures for the agreement.

Funnel Management

The concept of funnel management is that the customer (or project) acquisition process can be described as progressing through a series of phases. By tracking the behavior of "closes" as they traverse through the phases, one can identify a historical hit rate for proceeding from phase to phase. Thus, if it is noted that 20 prospects are required to get one sale, then, if two sales are required to meet the needs of the forecast, 40 prospects need to be in the prospect pool. The power of the funnel management concept is in its ability to monitor the effectiveness of the sales cycle and to generate forecasts.

Sell

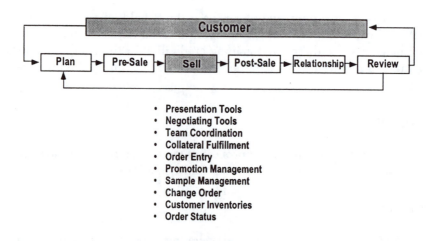

Figure 4.4   Sell cycle within the sales process.

The sell phase of the sales cycle moves the process on from quoting to actively engaging the customer in making the sale happen. The sell phase ends when the product arrives or the service is engaged.

Presentation Tools

Presentation tools are related to sales tools. The difference is essentially the choices or capabilities of the salesperson to present proposals or other relevant value-added information to lobby for the business.

Negotiating Tools

These are tools that help the salesperson effectively deal with a negotiating counterpart on the customer's side. It includes any approval processes involved.

Team Coordination

Team coordination covers those complex selling situations where a selling team is employed.

Collateral Fulfillment

Collateral fulfillment is a process that consists of field requests for specific reports or materials that are used by the salesperson to add value to the customer, facilitate the specification process, reinforce a claim made by the company, or otherwise inform the customer.

Order Entry

Order entry covers the process of conveying the order to a point where it is formally entered into the corporate order system and the system acknowledges the receipt of the order and confirms the desired delivery date.

Promotion Management

Promotion management pertains to those industries (e.g., consumer goods) that discount products or services on a regular basis. Promotion management is a process of managing the promotion offering in the field and assessing its effectiveness.

Sample Management

Sample management can involve very detailed monitoring of samples due to legal requirements or high value. In this respect, the issue is one of inventory management. Another aspect of sample management could be tracking the success rate of samples leading to new business. In this context, the issues are similar to lead management—are the samples driving the business?

Change Orders

Change order is the internal process by which an order in the system can be modified.

Customer Inventories

It is becoming increasingly prevalent for suppliers to provide customers product on consignment or otherwise hold inventory (safety stock) for the customer at no cost to the customer. Regardless of the location, some mechanism must be in place to report on withdrawals from inventory and periodically verify the counts. Sometimes it is the salesperson who does the count. In other cases, the salesperson needs to be apprised of the situation.

Order Status/Logistics

The salesperson is expected to know the status of an order throughout the cycle and specify when it will be delivered.

Post-Sale (Figure 4.5)

Billing/Accounts Receivable

Concerns on the part of the salesperson are that invoicing is accurate and complete and that bills are being paid. Monitoring these processes is the main concern of the salesperson. If there are discrepancies, the salesperson is often requested to help reconcile the problem.

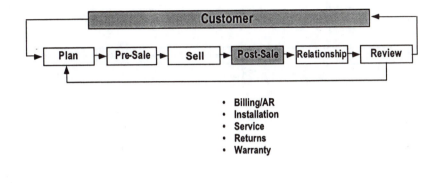

Figure 4.5   Post-sale phase of the standard sales cycle.

Installation

During the installation phase, the salesperson needs to be apprised of the status of the work and any complications that develop. The salesperson may be involved in helping the customer to facilitate the installation.

Service

In many situations, the salesperson is interested in knowing when service was required and the status of the call. Some companies have given their salespeople the ability to monitor equipment at the customer's site. The rationale for this ability is that the salesperson can help to assist the customer to maximize the use or effectiveness of the supplier's product.

Return/Warranty

A salesperson is often asked to complete paperwork associated with returns or warranty-related requests. At a minimum, the salesperson initiates the paperwork for such transactions. If not directly involved, the salesperson needs to be informed of all such transactions.

Relationship Building

Over time, it is the objective of sales to cement a relationship with key accounts so that they will represent a steady and reliable source of future

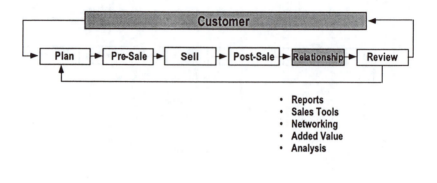

Figure 4.6   Relationship building.

revenue and improved margins. This is accomplished through a process of personal networking within the customer's organization and through a process of adding value to the customer that is recognized by the customer's organization (Figure 4.6).

Reports

Reports are essential to relationship building because they assist the salesperson in looking for trends and opportunities that can help the account improve. Obviously, reports must be timely and credible from the customer's perspective; otherwise, the salesperson is left to gather information on his own, which is wasteful and can lead to questionable practices in the field.

Sales Tools/Analysis/Networking

The topic of sales tools was identified in the discussion of pre-sale activities and requirements. In this phase of the process, the sales tools need to provide the salesperson with information or analysis that will be of interest to people outside the normal contact level of the salesperson. The intent of this information is to position the salesperson as adding value and to provide greater insight regarding the direction of the customer. Whether formalized or not, the intent is to develop a partnership that will favor the supplier in future purchase transactions.

Review

The review phase represents two sequential steps. The first step is to schedule review meetings with the customer. The objective of the review meeting is to communicate the level of business completed during the year, highlight value-added activities, report on levels of performance maintained in servicing the customer, and secure their feedback. The review should also seek to identify the customer's perspective regarding their markets and their strategic direction. The customer's sense of priorities should also be sought. This is key input to the supplier's organization at large and to the development of specific plans for the account. The review step is an excellent opportunity to introduce senior managers to the account and perhaps members of corporate staff functions.

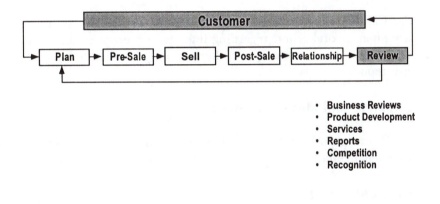

Figure 4.7   Review phase of the sales process.

Review Meeting

This step really is a compilation of capabilities outlined previously. In addition to effectively probing for the direction and priorities of the customer, the meeting reinforces the quality of the performance of the supplier and reaffirms the mutual benefit of working together. If there are problems, the meeting may help to gain better insight or state each side's perspective. The discussion may lend insight regarding competitive moves that are not apparent in the marketplace.

Communication

The supplier organization needs an easy method to distill the content of the review meeting so that others in the supplier's organization can share this same insight.

Administration

From a workload standpoint, a parallel activity to the sales process is administration. Administration is typically associated with a series of forms and involves field management and corporate functions. Examples of these processes follow.

Call Reporting

Call reporting or itinerary reporting involves the submission of either a written or oral report regarding intended coverage or the content of actual calls. In some cases, a weekly summary is submitted in place of a call report.

Expense and Mileage Reports

These reports document expenses incurred in the field and the maintenance of the company car or other lease arrangements.

Request Forms

These forms include requests for more forms! Typically, applications involve requesting literature, samples, sales tools, reports, assistance, etc.

Personnel Forms

These forms could include "out-of-the-field time," vacation requests, etc.

Summary of the Model

This model is oriented at comprehending the management of all aspects of the sales function:

■ Resource management

■ Customer interface

■ Customer acquisition process

■ Delivery of value to the customer

■ Interfaces with internal resources

■ Maintenance of the customer relationship

■ Methods to increase strategic leverage within the marketplace

The importance of the model, other than organizing the various facets of sales, is that it incorporates the moments of truth in the context of the sales effort. Chapters 2 and 3 addressed the need to do these things well, and this model starts to form the framework for understanding how to make it happen. Chapter 5 ties these concepts together in the form of organizational alignment. Once the alignment concept is defined, it is then possible to comprehend the full potential strategic value of sales force automation.

CHAPTER 5

INTEGRATING THE MODELS: DELIVERING VALUE

The Alignment Concept

Chapters 3 and 4 outlined two basic models for viewing the interface between the supplier and customer organizations. The model in Chapter 3 emphasized the concept that the processes which touch the customer represent horizontal transactions as opposed to vertical processes. Since most corporations are built on vertical functional principles, it is very easy to see why this structure complicates business and leads organizations to seek out new structures. The model in Chapter 4 expanded on the classical view of the sales process, which often limits itself to customer acquisition. The sales process model also provides another view of the interplay between the sales process and internal support processes.

The customer responds to the net of these processes. Depending on the nature of the customer's business, structure, and strategy, some areas of performance will receive a higher weight than others; the challenge is to define the mix of customers and performance levels that maximize growth and profitability.

In physics, the concept of "vectors" is used to describe the nature of force. Graphically, a vector is described as an arrow; the length of the line is proportional to the strength of the force, the angle of the arrow indicates its direction, and the arrow points in the direction that the force is being applied. If this concept was applied to the net force (value) experienced by the customer, the diagram might appear as represented in Figure 5.1.

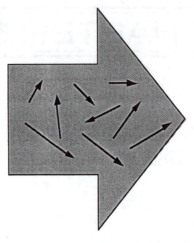

Figure 5.1   Organizational impact with non-alignment.

In the figure above, the arrows are pulling in different directions. This is not necessarily a sinister situation; it could merely reflect internal policies and procedures that are not aligned with what's important to the customer. The net of this situation is a shortened aggregate vector that gets the job done, but at what cost for the supplier and with what impact for the customer? Taking this same concept forward and aligning the effort of the organization, it is reasonable to project the diagram in Figure 5.2.

In this case, the arrows are all going in the same direction; thus the length of the aggregate vector is longer, indicating greater impact. At the same time, the aggregate vector is more narrow, indicating less cost due to a congruence of objectives within the supplier organization. Thus, this arrangement generates maximum force (value) at minimum cost to the supplier. In practice, it may not be feasible to get perfect alignment. However, it should be possible to significantly reduce costs, particularly if there is a high level of misalignment in the process. When one considers the hoops that are often associated with getting things done, this is not hard to believe. This is really the foundation for reengineering and the reason why one can expect to achieve order of magnitude improvements.

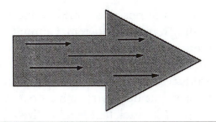

Figure 5.2 Perfect organizational alignment.

The remainder of the chapter will outline these concepts in greater detail using typical processes to make the ideas more real.

Defining Value

Value Concepts

Value used in the context of a purchase decision implies some type of conversion of the attributes of the item into a corresponding cost (price). Since business-to-business vs. consumer purchases involve different types of personal motivation, the following discussion will be targeted at business-to-business purchase decisions. In this context, many authors have incorporated the term into their writings. Some authors have chosen not to define the term, while others have defined it in terms of cost or personal preferences.

In the past ten years, the term "value" has become as commonplace in business terminology as "quality" and "productivity" were in the past decades. As a reflection of the emerging importance of this concept, the American Marketing Association labeled the 90s as the "Value Decade."[1]

Traditionally, value has been defined from an organization's standpoint as the quality built-in a product or service relative to its price. Total customer value could then be described as a state in which the quality of the total experience, as perceived by the customer, exceeds its cost.

Economists define value as value "in exchange" (which implies the price commanded in exchange for goods and services), value "in use" (the function that a product or service performs which, in turn, satisfies some users' needs or wants), and "esteem" value (the prestige or psychic gratification associated with a product or a service).

In the parlance of the business world, value is associated with the price that one is willing to pay for an item. Competitive advantage is then defined as providing superior value at a lower net delivered price than anyone else in the marketplace. In business-to-business transactions, positioning of product and services is often done in the context of delivered or net costs, but this perspective does not include the value provided by firms, such as Intel, that legitimatize a product by announcing "Intel Inside." Thus, value is more than cost effectiveness; value can embrace the whole issue of competitiveness. Since competitiveness is not easy to measure, a reasonable surrogate is profitability.

A Definition of Value

The term value has basically three components:

1. The degree to which a supplier's product or service contributes to the salability of the customer's product or service. Examples of this could include "Intel Inside" or "Made with Hershey's Chocolate" labels on products.

2. The net cost benefit that a supplier's product or service has vs. other alternatives available to the customer including in-house manufacture.

3. The bias of the purchaser relative to personal or institutional needs.

Items 1 and 2 in totality can be addressed by the concept of contributing to the customer's profitability. The profitability concept is also consistent with the idea of partnership where two firms work together to the mutual benefit of both. The third item represents the softer aspect of value that is tied with psychological characteristics. Even in the business world, there are criteria used in the procurement process that are not related to profitability or even risk but, nevertheless, are weighted into the decision. For example, there may be a bias to purchase items from a Fortune 500 company rather than a smaller independent firm, because such a decision is not likely to be second guessed. Thus, there is a second component to value which pertains to any intrinsic characteristic of the supplier that meets the personal need of the buyer.

For the purposes of this text, the term "value" will be interpreted as follows:

■ Value is a function of how a product/service contributes to the profitability of the customer's operation.

■ Value can also be an intrinsic characteristic of any aspect of the supplier that meets the personal need of the buyer(s).

Strategic Perspective

Another more financial format for this definition of value is as follows:

Supplier Value Contribution	=	Revenue Improvement Potential for the Customer	−	Total Costs of the Customer
		Competitive advantage		Delivered cost
		Supplier image		Net price
		Design		Freight
		Technology		Insurance
		Cost savings		Unloading/handling
		Material handling		Acquisition costs
		Inventories		Negotiation
		Financial terms		Invoice handling
		Manufacturability		Communication
		Maintenance		Logistical coordination
		Training support		Follow-up
		Setup features		
		Scrap/defects		
		Return policy		
		Intrinsic characteristics		

Note that the definition embraces product, services, market leverage, and the customer's internal costs. The value perspective must be a "big picture" view of the relationship. This perspective also helps to test the notion of a business model because it challenges the organization to determine if value and price are going in the same direction or remain proportional to one another. Failure to keep value and price in the right relationship is a sure sign of vulnerability to a different business design.

Another way of positioning this definition of value is to segment value via a relational perspective as follows:

Direct Value	Integrated Value	Strategic Value
Increased revenue	Improved service level	Improved processes
Increased sales	Increased productivity	Reduced cycle time
Cost reduction	Increased market share	Improved quality
Rework reduction	Reduced variation	New markets
Cost avoidance		New products

This perspective provides a good summary of "what" could be potentially leveraged, but it does not provide any definition of how or where to improve.

Having defined value in this manner, it is now possible to examine the procurement and use process from the customer's perspective and draw some reasonable conclusions regarding issues from their perspective. This perspective will then be tied to the processes that touch or impact the customer. In this manner, it will be possible to describe how the models presented in Chapters 3 and 4 actually can be used to study the issue of alignment.

Basic Customer Processes

The following items provide a generic list of processes and concerns from a customer perspective:

Procurement

■ Important characteristics:
  ❖ Product meets specifications
  ❖ Broad product line
  ❖ Actual performance meets specifications
  ❖ Reliable supplier who has the capacity to meet requirements

- ❖ Supplier with quality, regulatory, and manufacturing technology to meet specifications

- ❖ Specification information addresses issues or questions

- ❖ Questions answered quickly

- ❖ Clear pricing and terms

- ❖ Value-based pricing

- ❖ Knowledgeable salesperson who can make things happen within their organization

- ❖ Minimal lead-time relative to other options or the industry

- ❖ Salesperson who facilitates the internal buy cycle

- ❖ Image in the industry

- ❖ Contribution to marketing efforts

- ❖ Lack of hassles coming back from other areas of the company, particularly returns

- ■ Performance characteristics:

  - ❖ Reliability of the company doing what it says it is going to do

  - ❖ Reliability of the salesperson doing what he says he is going to do

  - ❖ Turnaround time for information and decisions

  - ❖ Competitive net applied cost

Design

- ■ Important characteristics:

  - ❖ Technical expertise

  - ❖ Reduced development cycle time

  - ❖ Resource and partner in the development of innovative solutions

  - ❖ Responsive to questions and troubleshooting

■ Performance characteristics:

   ❖ Applicability of recommendations

   ❖ Reliability of recommendations

   ❖ Turnaround time on recommendations designs, samples, etc.

   ❖ Technical updates and training

Use Within the Customer's Facilities

■ Important characteristics:

   ❖ Product/service meets specifications

   ❖ Clear labeling or references to facilitate manufacture

   ❖ Reliability and failure rates

   ❖ Ease of diagnosing problems

   ❖ Manufacturability and process yield

   ❖ Handling and setup costs

   ❖ Scrap rates and costs

   ❖ Waste and/or by-products generated

   ❖ Flexibility (ability to apply to more than one application)

   ❖ Breadth of product line (uniform product and user knowledge)

   ❖ Inventory requirements based on delivery cycle and reliability of supply/delivery

   ❖ Contribution to employee training

■ Performance characteristics:

   ❖ Positive impact on direct and indirect costs

   ❖ Quality statistics

Administrative

- Important characteristics:
  - ❖ Accurate and complete paperwork
  - ❖ Paperwork organized to facilitate the customer's processes
  - ❖ Turnaround time for answering questions
  - ❖ Speed of resolving issues
  - ❖ Use of electronic communication and transactions
  - ❖ Easy warranty and return processes
- Performance characteristics
  - ❖ Cost of doing business

Receiving

- Important characteristics:
  - ❖ On-time delivery (note this can vary from days to literally minutes depending on the item and the industry)
  - ❖ Properly marked
  - ❖ Easy handling and protection from damage
  - ❖ Paperwork is complete and easy to understand
- Performance characteristics:
  - ❖ Timeliness **as measured by the customer**
  - ❖ Cost of handling

Strategic

- Important characteristics:
  - ❖ Contribution to the organization relative to trends in the industry, technology, techniques, regulatory considerations, etc.

■ Performance characteristics:

   ❖ Presence of service management

   ❖ Perceived quality and insight provided

Marketing/Merchandising

■ Important characteristics:

   ❖ Perceived contribution to stimulating demand or generating higher margins

   ❖ Marketing partnership/expertise availability

■ Performance characteristics:

   ❖ Contribution to growth

   ❖ Contribution to revenue

   ❖ Contribution to margin

Risk

■ Important characteristics:

   ❖ Financial stability

   ❖ Commitment to the business

   ❖ Commitment to quality

   ❖ Commitment to leadership

   ❖ Commitment to customers

   ❖ Labor relations

   ❖ Litigation issues

■ Performance characteristics:

   ❖ Non-interruption of business

Supplier Processes

After defining the customer's processes and priorities, the next logical step is to map the supplier's interfaces and processes that impact performance as viewed by the customer. Since these interfaces vary considerably by industry, a composite view will be presented in this section to provide a flavor for this analysis.

Procurement

Customer Process: Procurement					
Supplier Processes by Functional Group					
Marketing/Sales	Management	Technical	Mfg./Distribution	Customer Service	Financial/Legal
Pricing	Empowerment	Design	Flexibility	Order Entry	Terms
Lead Mgmnt.	Turnover	Demos	Order Cycle Time	Order Status	Credit
Channel Mgmnt.	Policies	Problem Solving	Quality	Change Order	Contracts
Presentations	Hiring	Specifications	Scheduling	Inventory Status	
Literature	Incentives	Manufacturability			
Field Training					
Product Mgmnt.					
Sales Tools					

Comments

The real issue in the procurement process is being easy to do business with. Are cycle times short and is the organization responsive to the questions and steps associated with the customer's internal procurement steps? Channel and lead management are relevant here because lead management should qualify leads to ensure that the field is following up on viable business. This reduces response time for qualified leads. Second, channels should be aligned to meet the needs of the customer; incorrect channel alignment will result in dissatisfied customers and margin erosion. Order entry and tracking are critical to ensure delivery of the correct product/service at the right place and at the right time. In many cases, the salesperson must orchestrate the customer's internal procurement processes because they may not articulate their own internal value needs within the organization. In some cases, technical expertise can be the critical factor in the procurement process, particularly where the customer is trying to reduce product development lead times;

the supplier with a viable solution first often has a significant leg up on the competition.

Design

Customer Process: Design					
Supplier Processes by Functional Group					
Marketing/Sales	Management	Technical	Mfg./Distribution	Customer Service	Financial/Legal
Pricing	Empowerment	Design	Flexibility	Installation	Terms
Product Mgmnt.	Turnover	Demos	Order Cycle Time	Field Services	Credit
Channel Mgmnt.	Policies	Problem Solving	Quality	Inventory Status	Contracts
Field Training	Hiring	Specifications	Scheduling		
Product Dev.	Incentives	Manufacturability	Innovation		
Sales Tools		Responsiveness			

Comments

For most suppliers who provide their customers with unique designs or services, the desired competitive position is to be considered an extension of the customer's staff and participate in the design of the customer's product or service. The advantages of such a position are as follows:

■ The customer's focus will be on utility and value added rather than price.

■ It is unlikely that the item will be involved in a bid process.

■ The supplier can hone their services based on these processes.

■ The supplier has superior insight regarding the direction and needs of the industry.

■ The supplier has superior insight regarding emerging technologies or potential substitute products/services.

■ The supplier can influence the specifications to favor their strengths.

■ Success rates in terms of providing designs, samples, and proposals will be significantly higher.

■ Net development effort will be more efficient and market driven.

To gain the level of trust and credibility needed to participate in the design process requires assuring consistent performance and, in some cases, going above and beyond expectations to deliver against crisis conditions. Thus, the organization must be aligned to provide superior performance on a regular basis and be prepared to go above and beyond when customers need this level of service. In the short term, this may incur higher costs but in the long term, core profitability and stability will be greatly enhanced. All of this activity and commitment must be built around a customer-oriented philosophy and operating objectives. The sales process must also be built on the premise that customers are to be moved toward this partnership relationship.

Component Use

Customer Process: Component Use					
Supplier Processes by Functional Group					
Marketing/Sales	Management	Technical	Mfg./Distribution	Customer Service	Financial/Legal
Product Mgmnt.	Empowerment	Design	Flexibility	Installation	Terms
Channel Mgmnt.	Turnover	Demos	Order Cycle Time	Field Services	Credit
Field Training	Policies	Problem Solving	Quality	Inventory Status	Contracts
Product Dev.	Hiring	Specifications	Scheduling		
Sales Tools	Incentives	Manufacturability	Innovation		
Industry Expertise		Responsiveness			

Comments

Whereas the "Design" process pertains to how the product/service operates within the customer's product/services "Component Use" is focused on internal manufacturability and the customer's operations. It would be expected that the design would incorporate manufacturability issues, but this may not be completely the case. For example, design of the supplier's shipping container may not be specified during design, but in working with operations people, a design may evolve that facilitates handling, changeover cycle time, or minimizing overwrap. In this regard, the salesperson, and perhaps customer service, are likely sources of supplier input regarding these ideas. Again, alignment of the organization in such areas as training, incentives, and the sales process must be consistent with delivering these capabilities.

Administration

Customer Process: Administration					
Supplier Processes by Functional Group					
Marketing/Sales	Management	Technical	Mfg./Distribution	Customer Service	Financial/Legal
Pricing	Empowerment	Design	Flexibility	Order Entry	Terms
Channel Mgmnt.	Turnover	Demos	Order Cycle Time	Order Status	Credit
Literature	Policies	Problem Solving	Quality	Change Order	Contracts
Field Training	Hiring	Specifications	Scheduling	Inventory Status	Invoicing
Sales Tools	Incentives	Manufacturability		Warranty	
				Returns	
				Product Service	

Comments

Administrative processes encompass all of the paperwork, interfaces, and policies that are normally associated with the sense of "ease of doing business." This implies flexibility, empowered people, accuracy of information and documents, turnaround time, and attitude. Policies and incentives need to be reviewed to ensure that desired behavior is reinforced throughout the organization.

Receiving

Customer Process: Receiving					
Supplier Processes by Functional Group					
Marketing/Sales	Management	Technical	Mfg./Distribution	Customer Service	Financial/Legal
Channel Mgmnt.	Empowerment	Design	Flexibility	Order Entry	Terms
Product Mgmnt.	Turnover	Demos	Order Cycle Time	Order Status	Credit
Sales Tools	Policies	Problem Solving	Quality	Change Order	Contracts
	Hiring	Specifications	Scheduling	Inventory Status	
	Incentives	Manufacturability			

Comments

The receiving process could probably be folded into the "Use" or "Administrative" processes outlined above; however, it has been separated to address a fairly rampant view within many organizations. It is common for organizations to hold the opinion that if they ship on the day they say they are going to ship, this constitutes meeting the customer's needs relative to delivery. In practice, customers may be managing delivery to the hour or less. Obviously, shipping on the predicted "day" says nothing about meeting the customer's needs or expectations. In some cases, difficulties or limitations lie within available systems; in other cases, attitudes regarding shipment criteria are influenced by manufacturing's desire for more flexibility to gain economies of scale. Failure to address this area will frustrate the customer, result in higher costs for the customer, and blind the supplier organization to address manufacturing performance issues.

Strategic

Customer Process: Strategic					
Supplier Processes by Functional Group					
Marketing/Sales	Management	Technical	Mfg./Distribution	Customer Service	Financial/Legal
Channel Mgmnt.	Participation	Design	Flexibility	Services	Terms
Presentations	Empowerment				Credit
Product Mgmnt.	Turnover				Contracts
Sales Tools	Policies				
Business Reviews	Hiring				
	Incentives				

Comments

As a supplier, to be included into a customer's strategic process is an enormous competitive advantage. Not only does one gain insight regarding the customer, but also the industry. In addition, this insight can provide a vital advantage in terms of lead time to respond to these needs. The sales process must be geared toward this purpose, but there must also be alignment within the supplier's organization to deliver service such that the customer will be inclined to move the relationship toward a partnership arrangement. If the customer does not offer this initiative, then it is in the supplier's best interests to promote business reviews with the customer's staff, particularly senior management. The purpose of the business review should be threefold:

- Review the business relationship from a historical perspective with particular emphasis on value added. Failure to do this places complete reliance on the customer's organization to communicate this internally; that can be a very dubious assumption.

- Review expectations regarding moving the business forward. This will help to gain commitment and set near term expectations regarding improvements.

- Review the customer's perception of the industry, how they compete, and what their priorities are. This provides insight regarding the supplier's own strategies.

Participation by the supplier's senior management across functional lines is critical to leveraging this insight. This does not mean that senior management must be involved with every review, but, certainly, they must be involved with key customers and those who are considered the movers and shakers within the industry.

From a strategic perspective, the supplier needs to gain an understanding of their customers' direction, which implies defining:

- Customer organizational goals

- Critical success factors

- Internal organizational obstacles

- Market obstacles

The supplier must be able to take this information and develop solution strategies and map their impact. This represents a true external approach to the market.

Marketing/Merchandising

Customer Process: Marketing/Merchandising					
Supplier Processes by Functional Group					
Marketing/Sales	Management	Technical	Mfg./Distribution	Customer Service	Financial/Legal
Pricing	Empowerment	Design	Flexibility	Order Entry	Terms
Promotion Mgmnt.	Turnover	Demos	Order Cycle Time	Order Status	Credit
Advertising	Policies	Problem Solving	Quality	Change Order	Contracts
Channel Mgmnt.	Hiring	Specifications	Scheduling	Inventory Status	
Presentations	Incentives	Manufacturability			
Literature					
Field Training					
Product Mgmnt.					
Sales Tools					

Comments

This process addresses those situations where the supplier's name, brand name, or marketing programs leverage the customer's business either directly or indirectly. Examples would include "Intel Inside" stickers on computers or Kraft-General Foods merchandising programs in supermarkets.

Despite the fact that the sales function reports to marketing in many companies, there is an astonishing lack of market segmentation of customer sales and service preferences. Indeed, this is a major opportunity for marketing to add value to the sales function.

Risk Reduction

Customer Process: Risk Reduction					
Supplier Processes by Functional Group					
Marketing/Sales	Management	Technical	Mfg./Distribution	Customer Service	Financial/Legal
Pricing	Empowerment	Design	Flexibility	Order Entry	Terms
Lead Mgmnt.	Turnover	Demos	Order Cycle Time	Order Status	Credit
Channel Mgmnt.	Policies	Problem Solving	Quality	Change Order	Contracts
Presentations	Hiring	Specifications	Scheduling	Inventory Status	
Literature	Incentives	Manufacturability			
Field Training					
Product Mgmnt.					
Sales Tools					

Comments

Risk is the type of term that typically takes on a negative connotation; however, suppliers can leverage a low risk (as defined by the customer) profile as a means to garner a premium margin, maintain partnerships with highly valuable customers, or both. From a sales standpoint, leveraging this strength or minimizing this liability is a function of supplying effective sales tools and training to position the issue correctly and back it up with tangible arguments.

Integrating the Ideas

What is being advocated here is a serious review of how customers are competing in their markets and how current and future products, services, and support could contribute to the customer's competitive efforts to the mutual benefit of both organizations. An important vehicle for achieving value for the customer is the alignment of effort throughout the organization to deliver customer-defined levels of performance. These aspects are summarized in Figure 5.3.

Referred to as a value chain, Figure 5.3 demonstrates the opportunities to add value and contribute to the customer's competitive capability. It should be apparent that without comprehending the entire value chain, it will be very difficult to identify opportunities past the initial production of the product. Once the value chain is understood, the next step is to implement methods that maximize value per unit of cost. The relationship is portrayed in Figure 5.4.

Sales force automation offers a set of tools that can contribute to the value/cost relationship, but achieving that potential is largely determined by the approach. As will be discussed, the capabilities of today's technology are impressive, and it is not difficult to conceive of some desirable wins for the sales force, but is this going to generate the basis for a competitive advantage? Competitors can duplicate technology; what they will have difficulty with is alignment and customer focus that are unique within the marketplace.

Chapter 6 initiates the discussion regarding sales force automation by providing a model of how the technology works. This will serve as a launch pad to discuss types of applications and the broader issues of planning and implementing a system.

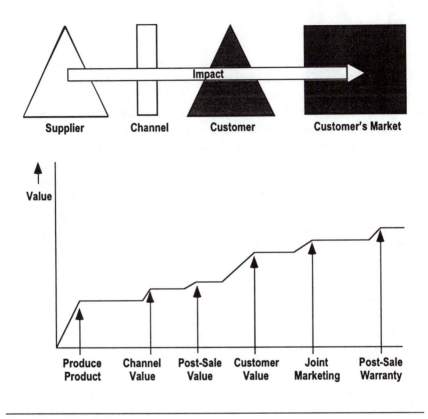

Figure 5.3   Value chain concept.

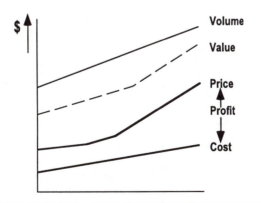

Figure 5.4   Value/cost/profit relationship.

Perspective

A decision to utilize sales force automation needs to be predicated on a business case that encompasses where the company is today and where it wants (needs) to be in the future. The models presented to this point provide a framework for defining both current and future states. The breadth of the view suggests that to complete it, in depth, one would have an assessment long after it was irrelevant. This type of delay need not be the case. The models provide insight regarding where to look and what to look for. In terms of customer impact, what is relevant is a sampling of customers, particularly those who are considered leaders in their industry or niche. Understanding their strategies will give insight regarding where the industry is going. Thus, the models provide direction; they do not assume that any organization has all the answers. Rather, the model should help to prioritize action.

Endnote

1. Edwin T. Crego, Jr. and Peter D. Schiffrin, *Customer Centered Reengineering* (New York: Irwin, 1995), 21.

CHAPTER 6

A CONCEPTUAL TECHNOLOGY MODEL

Technology as an Enabler

Chapters 1–5 have provided a conceptual model for competitive advantage through the delivery of superior value and margins. The emphasis has been on understanding the customer and how the customer views the product, service, and interfaces it has with the supplier organization. Fundamental to this concept has been the alignment of the organization behind the sales effort and the ability of the salesperson to deliver value to the customer. Although this issue has many facets, the models presented reflect the need to improve cycle times, the quality of information flows, and the range of capabilities of the sales effort.

To begin to understand the role that systems technology can play in this regard, a conceptual model for sales force automation must be established. The intent of this chapter will be to provide an overview of the elements of a system with emphasis on the user interface and general industry trends. This discussion will form the basis for Chapter 8, which will describe specific applications and the opportunities they represent.

The Network: The Backbone

The term *sales force automation* has been applied to a wide variety of stand-alone and networked systems. If one defines sales force automation as any software application that embraces the productivity of the individual salesperson, then all of the above apply. However, if the focus, as outlined in Chapter 1, is on delivered value to the customer, then the integrated effort of the company becomes a key capability. With the ability to network (i.e., the ability to share data and communication), software becomes a necessity.

Types of Networks

There are three types of networks, with many options associated with each. The three types of networks are LANs or local area networks, WANs or wide area networks, and VANs or value-added networks. As the name implies, a LAN connects devices in close physical proximity to one another, typically within a building. LANs use wire, coaxial cable, and fiber optics to make connections among the computers and other devices on the network. Wireless applications involving infrared rays are also possible. WANs span a larger geographical area than LANs. WANs employ telecommunications such as AT&T, MCI, Sprint, etc. Another form of a WAN is the PDN or public data network, which provides easy access and rates that are apportioned to usage. PDNs often use a transmission technique referred to as packet-switching, which basically breaks communication into fixed length units referred to as packets; this condensed traffic can be handled more efficiently across a WAN. A commercial network that adds services above the basic transmission capability (e.g., electronic data interchange, electronic mail, etc.) is referred to as a value-added network or VAN. WANs also have a wireless version; in this case, short wave transmissions are used to communicate between the user's device and a send/receive station; the station then connects the transmission to a ground-based WAN.

It is common for sales automation systems to utilize more than one type of network. For example, sales and corporate offices are likely to use a LAN to interface with the system vs. field users, who will utilize a WAN perhaps augmented by wireless. Integration with the Internet is also becoming increasingly common.

The Basic System Configuration

Figure 6.1 provides a schematic of a networked sales automation system. The field users are assumed to be using laptop computers that are connected with a server via a WAN. An optional wireless connection is represented by the field user on the far left of the diagram. Corporate users of the system connect with the server via a LAN. The server, in turn, supplies and receives downloads from the corporate databases. These databases could include inventory data, order status, leads, receivables data, etc. The database to the left of the server is dedicated to the sales and marketing functions and is designed to support decision making, analogous to a data warehouse concept. The PCs connected to the right of the server represent corporate users using a LAN network. The system

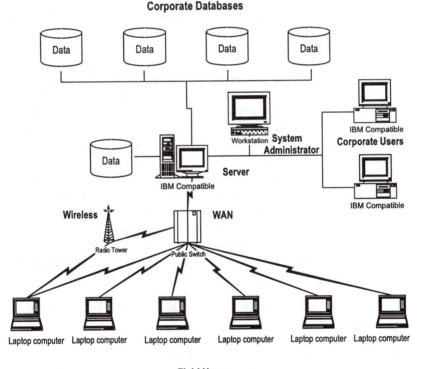

Figure 6.1   Basic network configuration assuming use of a LAN and WAN.

administrator connection serves as a reminder that these systems are dynamic in nature (part numbers change, accounts are traded among salespeople, and the software needs upgrading). Maintenance of the system requires added head count, and lack of timely and accurate updates will reduce confidence in the system and will lead to non-use. Field users are connected to the server through a WAN.

Most systems involving WANs utilize a store and forward concept for data transmission. As the name implies, a store and forward system is a batch method for transmitting data. The PC software is essentially free-standing in that it allows the end user to utilize its functions without being connected to the server. In the course of use, the system captures data as it is entered into the system and stores requests for mail, reports, reference material, etc. When the end user communicates using the WAN, the system recognizes all new information and requests and sends these to the server; the server automatically receives the data and hands the data off to the database while responding to mail requests, reports, etc. Thus, store and forward transactions tend to be of short duration.

The configuration includes a wireless connection to the server. Though the wireless connection is tied to only one laptop in the field, this does not imply that the capability is restricted to that one person. Indeed, where wireless is applicable, it is reasonable that it would be deployed across the organization. The advantage of wireless transmissions is that the user can connect with the server from any location as long as he is in range of a transmitter. Due to the higher cost of wireless, its use is generally limited to priority questions or issues that must be either sent/received as they occur or data that is highly time sensitive. An example of highly time-sensitive data could be available stock for unique products with long manufacturing lead times. In this case, the ability to confirm availability could represent a guaranteed order. Thus, the use of wireless transmission is typically associated with transmitting highly time-sensitive data that has the following characteristics:

- The data has cost implications for the supplier that are linked to lead time.

- The data adds value to the customer.

- The data has a high leverage effect on closing business.

Broad Benefits of the Configuration

The networked configuration is a powerful model that can reduce cycle times, leverage effort across the organization, and untether salespeople from support functions, thereby making them more responsive to the customer. The following items identify some of these key features:

■ **Data is fresh**: Depending on the communication medium, data can be as current as the moment (e.g., wireless).

■ **The quality of data is improved**: In addition to error detection protocol associated with data transmission itself, applications often assist the salesperson in the creation of accurate and complete data.

■ **Data availability**: The configuration provides ready access to accurate and relevant data regarding reference data, shipping dates, product availability, etc. This is true for the field, and it is true for staff and management functions. From a sales perspective, it means not being ambushed by a buyer regarding a late shipment or being able to answer questions immediately vs. follow-up; the difference can mean incremental sales.

■ **Communications costs**: By providing electronic messaging (mail) and timely data, less communication is required between staff and sales.

■ **Sales and support productivity**: As defined above, reduced communications costs are also reflected in higher personal productivity.

End-User Computer Devices

An enormous array of computer devices and accessories is available in today's market. The product life for laptop or notebook computers is so short that it is useless to comment on features except in the format of a periodical. Thus, this section will address basic concepts as opposed to specific capabilities.

The choice of a computer device for a field-based end user should be based on the applications and the environment the equipment will be exposed to. If a sales force consists of different functions (or levels) with significantly different responsibilities and applications/environment, then each function's needs relative to equipment should be considered as separate but connected decisions. Of particular importance is the type of interface. For example, if functional requirements involve input while standing, signature capture, or hostile environment (e.g., exposure to thermal or physical shock), the device should accommodate these conditions. For applications that require significant input while standing (consumer goods sales rep operating at the retail level), a pen-based product will be more functional than a device with a keyboard. Similarly, signature requirements suggests a pen-based interface. Environmental considerations may require a specially sealed or protected device. The message here is that consideration must be given to the physical interface, and if the field organization has different requirements due to levels or functions, then these needs must be considered as part of the overall solution.

Other physical characteristics include battery life and clarity of the screen under different lighting conditions. These are essentially usability considerations. Capacity and the ability to upgrade capacity or accessories (in a cost-effective manner) are also key considerations. To intelligently guide the purchase of field computers, there must be a strategic perspective regarding the type and size of applications over the life of the system (practical computer life cycle). Another consideration is the fact that most organizations will desire to maintain compatibility between personal productivity tools used in the office vs. those used in the field. This means that upgrades in the office must be matched with those in the field.

Choice of a manufacturer, features/capacity, and financing need to be considered as an integrated decision. In today's technology market where new computers have very limited product lives, it is possible to purchase very robust equipment at the $2,000–$3,000 level vs. the top of the technology ladder, which is 100–100+% higher. The choice ultimately gravitates to requirements that can be defined within the first two years of the system and how the organization wants to balance risk vs. investment in the remaining two to three years and beyond. One can configure an upgrade capability in terms of leasing or through component replacement. In developing this strategy, it is important to consider cost avoidance vs. disruption in the field if computers must be swapped out to accommodate these strategies. One final comment on this subject is that the decisions which are made relative to investment and risk will inevitably send a message to the field force.

Applications

The software that resides on the computers used by field sales and other people "linked" to the system is referred to as "applications." An application is a unique and complete set of software that has a specific purpose within the system. For example, a word processing package is an application, and order entry could be an application, etc. Types of applications will be discussed in greater detail in the next chapter; for the purposes of this chapter, it is important to be aware that applications form the capabilities of the system (from the user's perspective) to accomplish the tasks associated with the job. In this context, if the applications are appropriately selected and designed, sales reps will use them because the system assists them in getting the job accomplished.

An important attribute of applications is the user interface. If the interface is intuitive and the application works in concert with the salesperson, then it is more likely that there will be broad and appropriate usage of the applications across the sales force.

As positioned at the beginning of this chapter, **technology is an enabler**. Ultimately, it is the proper use of the system that creates competitive strength. Moreover, it is use of the system that establishes the ability of the organization to leverage future technology. If usage of the current technology is inconsistent, the sales force will not be in a position to leverage future, more robust technology.

The User Interface

The user interface refers to how computer screens are designed, how data is entered, and how one navigates through the system. These factors are very important to determining the actual use of the system in terms of breadth and depth across the sales organization.

One of the complicating factors in establishing a uniform and seamless interface is the co-mingling of off-the-shelf software with proprietary software developed or customized specifically for that sales force. Most corporate entities have standardized on word processor, spreadsheet, and presentation software. Thus, the challenge for the sales force is to learn these off-the-shelf packages, the customized software, and the methods for navigating within them.

Computer-related experience, particularly with more than one software package, facilitates the ability of users to bridge applications that have differing interfaces. However, if the user has limited to no prior experience in this area, the computer itself will be intimidating and different approaches and formats will be totally bewildering. Each sales organization will have a mix of computer use experience among its field membership. Over the past ten years, the percentage of experienced users has increased substantially, but the following profile (Figure 6.2) is fairly typical.

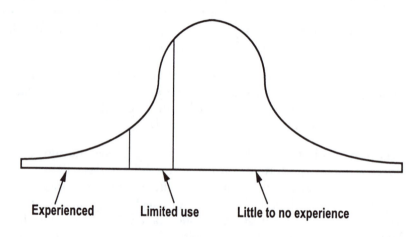

Figure 6.2   Typical distribution of personal computer experience within a field sales force.

Regardless of the experience level, each group has its challenges:

■ **Experienced Group**: Quite often, they do not understand why it has taken so long to provide technology to the sales force, and they want everything (applications) tomorrow. Often these people have purchased their own computers and software; if the standards for the system differ from their experience base, support from this group can turn to frustration at best and rebellion at worst. For this reason, it is desirable to involve these people in the design issues so that they can have "ownership" in these decisions.

- ■ **Limited Use Group**: This group is often an advocate for technology, but their focus is more on performing basic activities in a more efficient or quality manner. Thus, they lack the zealousness of the experienced group. Current experience with computer systems and applications is less of an obstacle for support, but there must still be sensitivity to addressing the relearning issue if it occurs. This group may provide valuable insight regarding the specification of fundamental capabilities associated with initial applications.

- ■ **Non-Users**: The most fundamental statement one can make about this group is that they have not established a strong enough definition of "what's in it for me" to invest in a personal system and learn it. The challenge for the user organization is to develop a compelling reason for learning and using the system.

Regardless of experience level, there is going to be learning, a change in the way processes are conducted, and new methods for communication. There must be a corresponding benefit to balance the personal investment. Management of this situation requires a combination of communication, system design, training, and application rollout strategy. Field communication is a constant demand regardless of the circumstances; however, as it relates to sales automation, a clear vision of where the organization is going and how it is going to get there is critical. System design relates to the user interface and other performance characteristics of the system. Training is a major consideration; quality training methods and adequate training time can impact the organizational learning curve, thereby reducing the personal investment required. Finally, the sequence with which applications are provided to the sales force must make sense to them, provide value (what's in it for me), and yet not overwhelm them from a learning perspective.

The point of this discussion is that software selection and system design have technical criteria, as well as a strong human element. One way to leverage acceptance and use of the system is to reduce the personal investment required to learn and use the applications. The following section outlines some general principles that reduce learning time (and sometimes performance time) as it applies to the user interface.

User-Friendly Design Concepts

The purpose of this section is to describe some basic considerations regarding the user interface. These concepts will prove very relevant to understanding the implications regarding the direction of the software market for sales automation.

- **Layout of the screens**: The screens should have a familiar look to them from a field sales perspective. Terminology should be consistent and the screens should not be crowded. Information should be grouped in a manner that the field will find logical and useful.

- **Uniform graphical interface**: To the extent possible, the look of the screens and basic interfaces within the system should be consistent. Use of icons and navigational methods should be uniform.

- **Data entry**: Wherever possible, data choices should be predefined and supplied as menu items. Edit checks built into the system should notify the user of inconsistent entries and/or missing data fields. If the same data is used in several places in the system, the system should automatically seed these locations.

- **Navigation across applications**: The system should operate intuitively; this implies the ability to cross applications without escaping or closing them out. This concept is portrayed graphically in Figure 6.3.

- **Communication with the server**: Inclusion of several off-the-shelf software applications can necessitate more than one communication session with the server. This condition adds complexity to the system and is sure to result in field-level frustration.

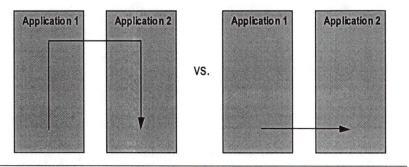

Figure 6.3   Navigation across applications.

The Human Element

All of this discussion boils down to one inescapable fact—it is the field user who must be the focus of the system. Technology alone is not going to provide a competitive advantage, certainly not a sustainable one. Ultimately, it is the people in the field and how they leverage the tools that are provided who will establish relative capability between competitors. For this reason, sales force automation is a complex amalgam of leadership, technology, management, and creativity. Ideally, one can liken the use of the system and competitive strength as a series of "S" curves:

The assumption regarding Figure 6.4 is that each generation of the system builds on the capabilities of the organization. Clearly, this can only happen when field salespeople are effectively utilizing each system as it is rolled out. Increased system robustness will not convert into competitive strength if the end users fail to embrace the system that preceded it. This does not forever condemn a company that fails on the first go round; it infers that proportional growth will be difficult unless the company gets it right.

In contrast, a corporation that does not effectively link the elements of leadership, technology, management, and creativity together will most likely experience the performance reflected in Figure 6.5.

Given these concepts as a model, the next section will provide a perspective regarding the sales force automation industry and trends that are likely to emerge.

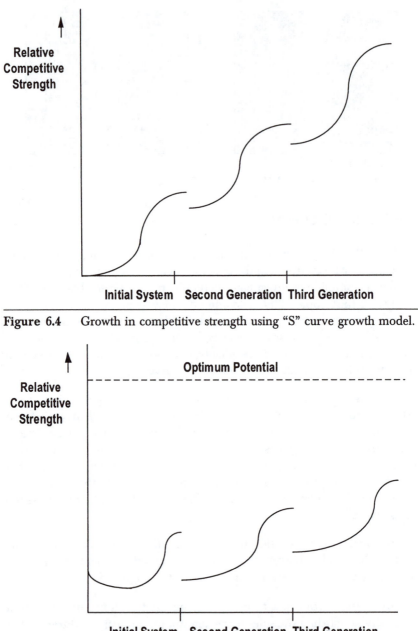

Figure 6.4   Growth in competitive strength using "S" curve growth model.

Figure 6.5   Restricted growth in competitive advantage due to inadequate field-user utilization.

Trends and Challenges for the Industry

Before embarking on a discussion of applications and their opportunities, it is appropriate to review trends and challenges within the industry. The following sections will provide a thumbnail sketch of the industry and implications of the current structure.

Background

The industry, as it applies to networked, field-based computer devices, started in the late 1970s. True laptop computers became available at reasonable street prices in the mid-1980s. The early innovators on the software side of the business had the daunting task of creating meaningful networked sales solutions in an environment where there was no precedent and certainly a lack of standards and inconsistent hardware designs. What emerged was a small group of venture capital-based software companies that developed a suite of proprietary products such as E-mail, territory management, and reports distribution that maximized performance, given the hardware and operating system limitations at that time. License fees were charged to use the software; this provided a mechanism to essentially pay for past investment and support the development of future releases. As initial customers purchased and installed these systems, it became obvious that the business did not simply consist of developing networked systems; customers needed services such as screen design and layout, a service bureau to run the system, training, help lines, and hardware prep/replacement. Business consultants, sensing a new niche, entered into the emerging disciplines and the issues they raised. Some system developers provided these services to their clients while others chose to seek alliances with third-party service providers.

Thus, like other innovation, the industry formed through the mutual learning of innovative suppliers and pioneering user corporations. It was the cooperative, and sometimes confrontational, linking of these organizations that formed the beachhead and fabric of the industry.

What few in the industry could have predicted was the rapid development of software and hardware capacity. With each increase in bandwidth came a corresponding demand for increased functionality. Given the license fee economic model, the relationship between license fees and development costs placed an enormous economic burden on system developers. The following graph (Figure 6.6) captures the relationship between lagging user fees and increasing investment and time costs associated with new product releases.

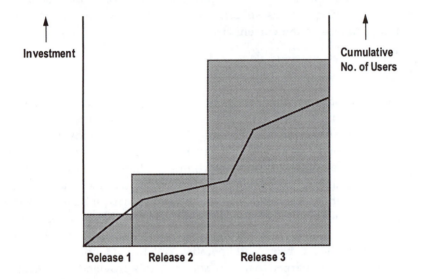

Figure 6.6   Relationship between release costs and time frames vs. user growth.

The time frame to release new versions of the software lags revenue substantially and requires disproportionately more time and investment to do so. In the interim, potential users delay purchase or seek another supplier who is closer to release of a new product. The practicality of maintaining a broad suite of products and upgrading the entire suite consistent with new operating systems has proven to be an economic impossibility. Consider the demise of some of the pioneers in the industry that followed this strategy.

Along with this rapid migration of software and hardware is the evolution of powerful shrink-wrapped versions of E-mail, forms, and reports generation software. In addition, some developers are providing what can best be described as middleware. The role of middleware is to provide an effective transfer link between the applications and their server. What has emerged, and will continue to evolve, is companies that specialize within industries and/or applications. They will seek to maintain

tain "best-of- breed" applications and offer these applications so they can interface in a number of environments and with complementary applications. Given this trend, it is likely that the market, from a technology standpoint, will consist of the following:

- Software developers (applications or packages)

- Specialists who develop custom applications

- Specialists who customize packages (e.g., opportunity management)

- Systems integrators who combine applications into an integrated system

- Turnkey project management specialists

- Consultants who recommend best-of-breed application packages based on the needs of the client

One of the challenges of this evolving marketplace will be to create the consistent and seamless user interface discussed earlier in the chapter. Fortunately, concurrent with these developments, object-oriented programming and object-linking concepts are providing the means to integrate best-of-breed applications into a best-of-breed system. This is exciting for the industry.

Trends and Challenges

The trend in the market today is for developers to concentrate on certain industries and/or specific applications. It is significantly more practical to develop and maintain a limited set of applications. The net result of all of these changes is that the capabilities of the industry have taken a quantum leap forward in the context of having a wide selection of applications, albeit at the cost of complexity. In the past, there were a limited number of suppliers who had a complete (figuratively speaking) suite of products. The dilemma was to select one supplier. Today, it is possible to choose the "best-of-breed" within each application; the challenge then becomes one of system integration and achieving the desired user interface. The positive news is that object-oriented programming is making this type of integration and seamless interface possible.

Brave New World: Same Needs

As one would expect in a technology-oriented industry, the only thing that doesn't change is change itself. However, the need for a solid understanding of business needs has remained constant; as a matter of fact, one could argue that with the greater diversity of choices and associated trade-offs, there is a greater need to know where you are going and why!

The rate of technological innovation continues unabated, and the same sense of restraint needs to be stated. It is easy to become enthralled by the bells and whistles and lose course. Evidence that this issue continues to haunt the industry is reflected in an article authored by Thayer Taylor entitled "Is Anyone Listening?"[1] In the article, Thayer cites a Culpepper and Associates' survey that indicates a rush to employ technology. These statistics reflect serious voids in understanding overall field needs and/or inadequate pilot evaluation. There is enormous vulnerability associated with overemphasis on application selection without consideration of system and process integration.

Complexity of the Industry

The industry really consists of a wide variety of goods and services. It is almost impossible to define a complete list of topics or areas of specialty. To make the point, consider the following.

- Hardware
    - ❖ End-users' computers
    - ❖ Printers
    - ❖ Servers
    - ❖ Hardware accessories (bar coding, modems, adapters, etc.)

- Software
  - ❖ Operating systems
  - ❖ Databases
  - ❖ Applications
  - ❖ Communications

- End-user-related services
  - ❖ Training
  - ❖ Help-line support
  - ❖ Hardware replacement and repair
  - ❖ Hardware preparation

- Network services
  - ❖ Land based (including Internet access)
  - ❖ Wireless

- Technology-related services
  - ❖ System design specialists
  - ❖ Customer development
  - ❖ Network specialists
  - ❖ System integrators
  - ❖ Application evaluation consultants
  - ❖ Service bureau (run server and manage network)

- Business-based services
  - ❖ Needs assessment
  - ❖ Reengineering
  - ❖ Sales-process specialists
  - ❖ Change-management specialists

With dozens and even hundreds of players associated with each category, the industry is fractious in every respect. The challenge for each end-user organization is to establish a clear direction for itself; otherwise it will get caught in the complexity and constantly changing face of the industry.

Endnote

1. Thayer C. Taylor, "Is Anyone Listening?" *Sales Process Engineering & Automation Review*, June 1995, 18–19.

CHAPTER 7

PUTTING THE PIECES TOGETHER

Overview

Thus far, a number of models have been developed that are intended to better understand the relationship between competitive performance and sales force automation. The discussion of each of these models was principally targeted at understanding the model itself; it is now possible to link these concepts together. This chapter will provide a brief review and then will integrate these models and perspectives. Given this linkage, it will then be possible to move ahead to a description of specific application types.

Sales Process vs. Customer-Value Models

The customer-value model emphasized the fact that the processes which directly interface with the customer are horizontal (organizational viewpoint) and, therefore, cut across functional lines. The concept of value was also presented by defining it in terms of profit contribution and fit with decision-maker agendas.

The sales process was defined as a series of major steps that are supported by a host of other support processes, the majority of which are horizontal in nature. The result is a composite view as described in Figure 7.1.

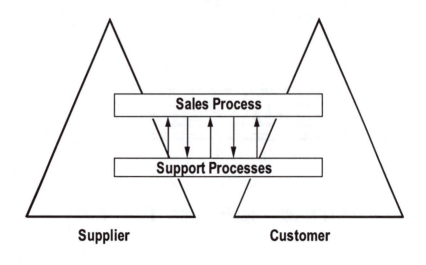

Figure 7.1   Integrated sales process and delivered value models.

The previous chapters also described the issue of alignment, which addresses the need to rally everyone and associated policies involved in a process toward the same end, so that maximum customer benefit is achieved at minimum cost and cycle time. The description of the sales process also included a discussion of how the salesperson can add value.

Leveraging the Processes

The conceptual model for a networked system emphasized the ability to exchange data rapidly and accurately among users on the system. The model also emphasized the need for user-friendly and intuitive interfaces to gain maximum organizational usage of the system. This chapter will expand on these capabilities of the system to leverage processes and deliver value to the customer. To demonstrate these capabilities, consider the three-step process reproduced in Figure 7.2.

The elements of the process are as follows:

- **Initial Input**: This is the trigger event for the process, whatever starts the set of events. It could be a request for a quote, it could be a lead, etc.

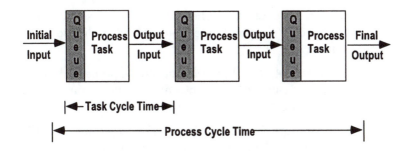

Figure 7.2 Three-step process illustration.

■ **Queue**: Each process step is preceded by a queue, which simply means a pending or holding state prior to actually being "processed" through the task.

■ **Process Task**: Specific steps or activities associated with completing a task.

■ **Output/Input**: The output of one process step becomes the input to the next. The orientation emphasizes the quality issue.

■ **Task Cycle Time**: The time required to move from receipt of an item, process it, and deliver it to the next task.

■ **Process Cycle Time**: The total time from the request (release) of the initial input to the delivery of the final output.

For simplicity, assume that the process and its associated steps or tasks are valid from a process design standpoint. How can the sales force automation system configuration shorten this process cycle, reduce costs, and increase value? Consider the following:

■ **Shorten Transfer Time**: If the input and output of each step can be placed in an electronic form, then transfer can be accomplished electronically and transfer times can be reduced from days to hours or even minutes.

■ **Shorten Process Task**: The length of a process task can be shortened by a myriad of techniques and applications. For example:

  ❖ **Reduce Administrative Content**: A properly designed system can seed data into documents, minimize data entry, automate calculations, etc.

  ❖ **Eliminate Reviews/Approvals**: Applications can integrate decision criteria and business perspectives so that the process task can include empowerment and eliminate steps. When this technology is aligned with proper incentive models, the result is more effective decision making (higher margins), and factor-effective decision making (higher margins), and faster processes.

  ❖ **Leverage Skill and Knowledge Levels**: Applications can provide guidance regarding recommendations (design capabilities) or may provide easy access and availability to reference information.

  ❖ **Quality Input**: Sales processes are notorious for incomplete and inaccurate data. Applications can provide a combination of menu selection and editing capabilities that force completion of required fields and help eliminate errors. This results in shortened process time and reduced costs.

■ **Manage Queues**: Ideally, a queue or pending status should be driven to zero. Certainly, the reduction in cycle time and increase in quality input/output will strongly influence the level or duration of pending time. However, when queues develop, this prioritization is necessary. Prioritization criteria can be built into the system so that high-impact items do not become stalled.

■ **Process Cycle Time**: Ultimately, it is the overall process time that should be of concern. In this regard, the system can be designed to identify throughput at each task level and the amount of time items have remained in any given queue. This type of information is key to establishing accountability at all levels; this includes management accountability for adding resources.

■ **Process Costs**: Given the suggested reductions in task cycle time, transfer time, and quality, it should be apparent that costs will follow proportionately.

■ **Process Integrity**: Process integrity pertains to the degree to which the process is followed and the reliability of the results. Applications need to be designed consistent with supporting critical processes. The design should "make it easy" to do the right thing and should reinforce best practices. Further, with built-in references and history, a process is less likely to suffer due to turnover in salespeople or other key functional areas.

Integrating the Concepts

As an enabling technology, sales force automation provides a means for leveraging key processes that touch the customer and add value based on the customer's criteria. These approaches include:

1. Extension of services to the customer through the sales force

   ■ Design capabilities

   ■ Market insight, supply side (e.g., commodity chemicals)

   ■ Market insight, demand side (e.g., consumer goods)

2. Solution orientation

   ■ Knowledge of the customer's business

   ■ Product selection

   ■ Economic decision models

3. Cycle time reduction

   ■ Pricing

   ■ Quotes

   ■ Special terms

4. Reliability

- Problem solving

- Ability to make things happen

- Accessibility

- Consistent quality and timely responses to questions

Examples

The next chapter will address sales automation on an application-by-application basis. Before entering that discussion, it may be useful to discuss value in the context of a process and how sales force automation can radically alter the power of performance associated with processes. The following examples are taken from real situations; they represent good examples of how sales automation can address internal and external value improvement. Since the next section will define applications in greater detail, the technology employed will be described in simple terms to provide an understanding of the nature and source of the benefit, without the detail of how these are accomplished.

Time Sheet

This example is taken from a customer service function for a major manufacturer of communications equipment. Field customer-service people are paid on an hourly basis with provisions for time-and-a-half and double time. Each week, the customer service rep must complete a time sheet that indicates time utilization and overtime qualification. The rep sends the time sheet to the manager via mail or fax. The manager is expected to review the time sheet and approve it, principally with regard to overtime. The manager must enter a computer system (via a terminal) and examine call history by account to determine consistency between the time on the call and that reported on the time sheet. Depending on travel schedule and other time demands, this verification process is spotty at best, and with travel schedules, the time sheets become delayed. Once signed, the time sheets are mailed to accounting, where they are entered into spreadsheets for analysis. Accounting then sends the time sheets to payroll, where they are entered into a another system for check issuance.

There are many problems with this process but among them are the following:

- Manual auditing to control synchronization between reported hours vs. paid hours.

- Managers must waste valuable time serving as auditors.

- The whole process stops due to availability of the manager.

- Double key entries can occur.

- Use of spreadsheets for analysis of data that should be in a database.

- Significant cycle time for the process (7–10 working days).

A sales automation solution for this process could include a territory management application that would contain all the accounts covered by the customer service rep. The call report section of the territory management could be used to record the details of the service call and to capture the duration of the call, which could automatically feed a time sheet application. Thus, these numbers would always tie out. At the end of the week, the time sheet could be sent to the manager electronically and the manager could receive it wherever he was at the time. Since the hours tie out, the manager could concentrate on issues such as utilization. Once approved, the time sheet could be electronically forwarded to accounting and payroll, where the data could be automatically uploaded to appropriate databases. This approach completely eliminates re-keying of the data and makes the data available within 24–48 hours. In addition to being more timely, the data should be more accurate.

Design of Prototype Electrical Components

This example is taken from a manufacturer of electrical components. In this situation, sales reps are asked by prospects and customers to quote on customized components required by OEMs. The sales rep gathers basic information and sends it to design people at the manufacturing plant. The design people create a design (typically modify standard components) and provide a price range for the sales rep.

If the customer approves of the concept, a prototype is made and sent to the customer for evaluation (this is normally done at no cost to the customer). Due to cycle time pressures on the OEMs, the first supplier with a workable solution often receives the business. The target cycle time for completion is three weeks, but it is often extended to five or more weeks due to communication delays and resolution of open issues.

The opportunity here is to create a method to speed up the prototype process to less than three weeks. Making the prototype was not the issue; delays occurred in getting the specifications right, which often took far too long because of the availability of the participants. Research had indicated a significant increase in revenue was probable if this time could be reduced.

The solution here is to develop a design configuration application that will allow a sales rep to develop a manufacturable design based on performance input from the customer. In this case, the design can be worked "in front of" the customer. In this manner, the customer can approve the concept, and the concept can be electronically sent to the plant for manufacture. Design people may have to review a few of the designs, but it should virtually eliminate their input. Turnaround time can be reduced to less than a week. In this case, the solution reduces costs while increasing revenue; it also positions the sales rep as adding substantial value to the process.

Extending the Concepts

The next chapter initiates a discussion regarding specific sales force automation applications and benefits. The remainder of the book will address the specifics of applications and how to develop and sell projects within the corporate environment.

CHAPTER 8

THE OPPORTUNITY

Integration of Focus and Effort

It is the thrust of this book that to maximize the impact of sales automation, organizations must start with the broader picture of delivering value to the customer. Although sales productivity and cost reduction have historically been achieved with a pure sales focus, the technology offers far too much power to limit the focus to the sales function or even sales/marketing. Thus, organizations are encouraged to take an external perspective regarding delivered value; this approach will facilitate thinking "outside the box" because this perspective minimizes myopic "four-wall thinking."

Though it may appear contradictory, the second major point regarding this technology is to pay attention to the sales rep in its design and implementation. This is not a new admonition within the industry; however, the rationale is somewhat different. Technology alone can be replicated by any competitor; competitive advantage is derived from how people utilize the system. Further, it can be argued that the ability to leverage future technology is tied to the utilization of current technology. On this basis, steps taken to ensure broad utilization and use of current systems have significant impact on future competitive capabilities. From a tactical standpoint, one would try to recoup the investment in the system as soon as possible, and this criterion is often used to judge the viability of an install. The problem occurs if high return applications are not correlated with encouraging or facilitating high usage rates. When this happens, a strategic perspective helps to keep focus on what the organization wants to achieve in the future. Having a longer term view and a vision for the organization ensures greater potential for doing the right thing as opposed to the expedient thing.

Lastly, it should be recognized that it is not practical or strategically sound to try to be all things to all customers. The supplier organization needs to be in touch with customer attitudes and priorities and then set a course regarding what areas it will excel in while merely maintaining a competitive parity in other areas. Clearly, this should guide the development of any system that is "delivered value" oriented. Not every customer is going to have the same priorities, and, therefore, the customer base will have differing levels of need regarding performance. As the capabilities come on board, to maximize margins it will be necessary to adjust the customer mix. The sales system should be viewed as a means for leveraging value and selling value as defined by the company's strategy.

This chapter takes the concepts presented earlier and positions them in the context of application capabilities. The sales model presented in Chapter 3 will provide the structure for this discussion. Since different industries will have different sales processes and needs, applications will be described from a number of perspectives.

Definition of Applications

Before attempting to link applications with the specific phases of the sales process, it is necessary to start with a basic understanding of application names and capabilities. These descriptions are intended to be generic and, certainly, the list will not be exhaustive. The purpose of the chapter is to provide insight regarding the capabilities of the technology and the impact the applications can have on an organization. Where practical, these applications will be placed in the context of strategic implications and value generation.

E-mail

This application allows mail messages to be sent to anyone on the system. The application is directly analogous to a post office. The server is a central repository for messages, and people send and retrieve messages from the server. Files can be attached to mail messages (e.g., letters, contracts, presentations, newsletters), thereby expanding the utility of the application. Electronic mail is complementary to voice mail in that electronic mail is text oriented, whereas voice mail is more context oriented. Bulletin boards can be set up with E-mail to serve as a way of sharing information with those who have an interest or requesting help for a problem where the source of assistance is not easily defined (e.g., a sales rep seeking help as to how to approach an emerging industry group might seek help from others in the organization who have experience with that industry).

Forms

Electronic forms is similar in nature to E-mail. Forms applications replicate paper-based or manual form processes. There are many features and advantages of the forms application:

- Elimination of paper forms, which means no printing, distribution, and warehousing costs.

- Reduction in mail or distribution costs.

- Quantum leap in transfer time reduction between process steps.

- Electronic signature reduces approval delays.

- Electronic editing and error reduction.

Dynamic Information Sharing

This application is a variant of electronic mail and forms. The difference with this application is that the intent is the sharing of information that is text based. The text can be "free form," or it can be organized in a database structure (e.g., a product reference file). This application is very flexible and can be used for open forum capability or specific structured sharing.

Contact Management

Contact management represents software that is specifically oriented to gathering and organizing information regarding individuals who are either prospects or customers. Calendaring and "to-do" functions are typically built in. Typical applications of this nature are integrated with a word processing package and have both profile and call history type of information imbedded in the system. Shrink-wrapped versions of the application often permit customization of certain fields, and some products permit sharing of information via electronic communication.

Territory Management

This application, sometimes referred to as account management, blends the tracking of information regarding prospects and customers in terms of corporate information and individuals within that corporation. There are shrink-wrapped and customizable versions of this type of application. This application also incorporates profile and call history (reporting) information. In addition, the application typically provides "sort and search" mechanisms that allow the user to view his territory from a number of perspectives, hence the title "territory management." It may also be possible to imbed a specific sales process methodology into the software, thereby making it easier to follow the discipline and enable uniform reporting relative to progress within the sales cycle.

Opportunity Management

This application is similar to territory management in concept; however, the focus of opportunity management is on managing sales opportunities. The software is therefore geared to managing priorities and making sure sales processes stay on track. Common to opportunity management systems is the ability to integrate team members into the sales process. Allied to this same principle is the ability to share calendars and assign tasks. These are critical capabilities in complex sales situations. Another feature of this approach is the ability to forecast sales directly from the opportunity manager. Although not unique to opportunity management, these applications typically integrate lead management into the whole.

Internet Reference

As an adjunct to contact, territory, and opportunity management, software suppliers are incorporating a direct link to web sites that provide financial and business information regarding suspects, prospects, or customers. This helps the sales rep to be knowledgeable regarding account issues while pre-planning calls.

Reports Distribution and Analysis

Although reports distribution and analytical capabilities are often two applications, it makes sense to discuss them in the context of complementary capabilities. Reports distribution consists of electronically sending pre-formatted reports to the field or sending data and providing the capability at the user level to convert the data into reports. Other software is available to allow analysis of the data through structured query or through more open-ended analytical tools.

Sample Management

Sample management is a specialized application that applies when the organization must (legal restrictions) or needs to manage inventory that is controlled by the sales force. The pharmaceutical industry is compelled to track drug samples due to legal requirements. Some industries provide inventory on a consignment basis due to its high cost (medical instruments), while others use samples as a means for closing business (paper industry). Typically, this is a custom or heavily customized application.

Order Entry

This application is often customized. The order entry application is used in situations where orders are submitted by the salesperson as opposed to being submitted directly from the customer. These applications will have built-in pricing and provide for the extension of all figures. They may include metrics that extrapolate full truck loads and other price break information. Inventory availability may be downloaded daily or be available through wireless connections.

Configurators

Configurators are specialized applications that generate complete bills of material level detail given basic input from a sales rep. The purpose of a configurator is to ensure a complete and properly priced quotation. The most recent configuration application releases push the threshold of sales assistance to the point of actually recommending solutions based on performance attributes as presented or described by the customer.

Proposal Generators

Proposal generators combine the attributes of several applications to form the basis for creating customized quotes and proposals based on limited initial input from the sales rep. This can include attachments such as contracts. Proposal generators can also be extended to respond to RFPs and/or RFIs.

Marketing Encyclopedias

These applications are built on database or multimedia (see next section) foundations. The encyclopedia is intended to provide background information regarding product usage, specifications, pricing, and competitive analysis/strategy. Some systems are directly linked with opportunity management systems.

Multimedia

This is an overall term given to applications that combine data, voice, and visual effects. This environment can be used for training, presentations, reference, etc. These applications can be very powerful as a sales tool.

Personal Productivity Tools

Personal productivity tools consist of shrink-wrapped software products that typically include word processing, spreadsheets, and presentation applications.

Forecasting

Forecasting tools range from statistical packages to spreadsheets that are updated by salespeople. A more user-friendly approach is being built into opportunity management software.

Mapping

Mapping software can be used for planning, analysis, and deployment applications. It can also represent a personal productivity tool in terms of locating prospects and pre-planning an itinerary. As an analytical tool, it provides the ability to visualize the geographical implications of data.

Linking Applications with Processes

Having described the elements of the sales process in Chapter 4 and having provided a brief description of typical applications, this chapter will describe the use of the applications to meet various types of sales process needs. Wherever possible, examples will be provided to add clarity and depth to the discussion. This chapter is titled "The Opportunity" because it is intended to demonstrate the economics and performance power of properly designed systems, as well as the diversity of applications of the technology. In this chapter, each sales process step will be explored in the context of how sales automation can leverage performance and value to the customer. This will provide a fairly complete discussion of need and capabilities in the context of the sales process model.

Planning Process

Starting with the plan phase, each of the applications will be discussed in the context of the sales process (see Figure 8.1).

Deployment

Deployment of a sales force is a multi-step process that starts with an estimate of the number of people required, their allocation to geographic boundaries, and, finally, the allocation of time to accounts and prospects.

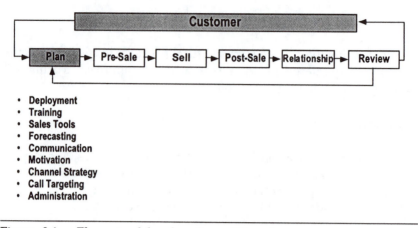

Figure 8.1   Elements of the plan phase of the sales process.

By its very nature, deployment decisions have a profound impact on productivity because it is an issue of aligning the right resources against the right opportunities. Even when equipped with superior tools, a poorly aligned sales force will dilute performance. Historically, this impact has ranged between 5% and 30%.[1] Andreis Zoltners, co-founder of ZS Associates in Evanston, IL, a consulting firm that specializes in realignment, estimates that 80% of the companies in the United States have imbalanced alignments.[2]

Although there are many techniques for addressing deployment, logically the decision process migrates from total number of people required to the specifics of assignment of accounts to territories. Within this process, one must make decisions regarding skill and knowledge levels, expected sales productivity, time requirements, and account or territory potential.

Sales automation can facilitate this process in a number of ways:

■ Call reporting and lead tracking are important sources of historical data regarding manpower utilization and "hit" rates for certain sales processes and methodologies. Paper-based systems are notorious for being incomplete and suspect in terms of accuracy. Automated call reporting and account management systems decrease administrative time associated with handling these tasks while increasing their timeliness and accuracy. Thus, the process starts with clean data.

■ Mapping applications can take the coverage and business potential data and produce a visual image that makes the allocation of responsibility (territory alignment) easier to develop. These applications can be combined with optimization routines to test the "goodness" of the alignment against pre-defined criteria.

■ Sales tools and training can be used to leverage the existing set of skills and knowledge available in the field, thereby reducing the need for sales reps traveling inordinate distances to cover unique accounts.

Realignment is not a static concept that only happens once during the life cycle of a company. Usually, it is an evolutionary process that is implemented in various stages to meet new customer or industry demands. For example, Air Products and Chemicals, Inc. of Allentown, PA, has reorganized its sales organization twice since 1990. Initially, they organized the sales force by product type vs. geography because product lines were not being given equal attention. Subsequently, they discovered a need to better understand their customer's industry. Thus, they came to the conclusion that sales reps needed to be deployed by product and industry. Some customers were not happy being called on by two salespeople; therefore, the company had to make accommodations. However, overall changes are credited with an 8+% growth in sales. Thus, sales forces that take the time to understand their customers and learn what they want or don't want are the ones that will succeed.

In a well-known and publicized reorganization, IBM redeployed its sales force around 14 industries and markets. The rationale—customers want solutions and people who understand their business. Customer surveys have since reinforced that this was a positive move.

Training

Sales training can be defined as the process of providing a salesperson or sales team member with the skills, knowledge, and attitudes necessary to increase that person's productivity.

The best sales training decisions are linked to an organization's key business objectives. Strategic sales training plays a role in supporting time-based competition by ensuring that strategies are communicated and executed quickly and consistently. Sales training should elicit the following characteristics:

- Sales training must be linked to sales strategy.

- Training must be designed, planned, and implemented to achieve specific objectives.

- Training must be implemented on a continuous basis.

- Training must be supported with follow-up and coaching.

- Sales policies and procedures must be consistent with the objectives of the training.

The cost of keeping a field sales force trained is staggering. There are transportation costs, housing, food, trainers, materials, and opportunity costs associated with having people out of the field. For large corporations, these costs average between $10,000–$25,000 depending on the industry. Short-cutting training also has its downside in terms of lost productivity, lost sales, and turnover of salespeople. Turnover alone can cost $50,000–$100,000 per occasion.

In recent years, a number of technologies have evolved that can effectively reduce some of these training-related costs. Video conferencing provides a means for salespeople to be trained at sites closer to their home, thereby reducing travel time and time out of the field. Using this technology, a live training presentation can be presented to a number of remote sites at the same time. An alternative is to video tape training sessions; the limitation with video tape is that it is not interactive. A more personalized form of training is possible through the use of interactive multimedia. Using this type of technology, the user can work at home or on the road. The training can pose situations and provide a variety of responses based on input from the user. The users work at their own speed, and the material can be reviewed as many times as necessary. For data or presentations that are not given on a regular basis, this training tool can be ideal because the material can be reviewed when needed; as such, it represents a form of "just-in-time training."

Jeff Howell, Director of Education for Andersen Consulting, says that the switch from traditional seminars to self study business practices courses is saving $10 million every year (travel and lodging).[3]

Interactive Learning trains Prudential sales reps. They now take 75% of their in-house training courses on their PCs or on special learning terminals. Previously, Prudential's training program was book and classroom based. New reps are expected to complete the core curriculum within the first 30 months of their employment with Prudential.[4]

Sales Tools

This category of applications is positioned within planning because the development of such tools must be an integral part of budgeting and planning as opposed to an afterthought. There are a wide range of applications that can potentially fall into this category:

■ **Multimedia**

❖ Companies are vying for more time with customers and better attention and retention from customers. Multimedia involves customers in the sales call and allows salespeople to customize presentations in minutes. For example, the air compressor group of Ingersoll-Rand has developed a presentation that contains extensive data on Ingersoll-Rand, its air compressors, and its competitors. The presentation includes the company history and animated air compressors, plus nine technical calculators to compute energy or cost figures. Closing ratios have been reported to have increased substantially. Multimedia makes intangibles more tangible and demystifies technical products for non-technical people. Presentations can contain information about the company, competitive data, price lists, delivery schedules, product specifications, and live testimonials.

❖ McDonnell Douglas Helicopter Systems, located in Phoenix, AZ, sells helicopters to commercial and private parties. The entry-level machine costs over $650,000, with the average helicopter selling at $850,000. There are over 500 options associated with any purchase. The company's sales automation system includes an account manager, digitized catalog with full motion picture video, and maps of supply depots worldwide. The multitude of parts options are handled by an animated technical description feature that has a rules-based structure which guides table prompts, thereby eliminating the potential for error in selection. A purchase order generator covers all the contractual details and creates contracts at the customer's site. A financial analysis application can set up a lease arrangement and can guarantee the price so that the sales rep can close the deal on the spot.[5]

❖ Toshiba America Medical Systems sells CT and MRI scanners. The products are very large, highly technical, and specs are changing constantly. To present product to customers, Toshiba developed a sophisticated interactive presentation with elaborate 3-D animation, high-resolution scans, and video clips of the product in operation, as well as narrated testimonials from satisfied customers. There is an architectural schematic showing the exact space requirements. Customer education is critical to the sales along with the education of the sales rep. Salespeople internalize the product by working with the demo.

■ Reference Information

❖ This information typically involves price information, product specification sheets, product literature, and competitive data. Reference-oriented applications eliminate the need for using three-ring binders, mailing stacks of literature to the field, and spending hours culling and replacing materials in the field. In addition, these applications have an easy interface to facilitate navigating through the material to quickly find the desired reference.

❖ Bergen Brunswig is an $8 billion distributor of drugs that supplies to pharmacists. They investigated sales force automation with the objective to differentiate the company and create loyalty among customers while reducing expenses and increasing sales revenue. The company created a product encyclopedia and presentation system for salespeople. It contains 12,000 products, details each pharmacy account status graphically, and links it to presentations on marketing programs. The pharmacists liked the information so much the company created a lease program for pharmacists. The system helps pharmacists make profitable decisions on every prescription they fill. It has generated more order volume because it is easy to use. Sales revenue is up 11%, and earnings are up 26%, while sales expenses have dropped as a percent of revenue.[6]

■ Design Capability

❖ It is difficult to find a company that is not trying to shorten its design and development cycles. From a sales perspective, it is often the supplier who has the first demonstrable solution that gets the business. Design applications can consist of (1) helping the salesperson to get all relevant facts before forwarding them to design engineers, thereby reducing fact-finding time or (2) the application may allow the salesperson to design the design while working with the customer.

❖ Wells Fargo Alarm Services, a Borg-Warner Security Company, was plagued by long turnaround time on quotes and extensive installation problems when equipment was not specified correctly or essential parts were missing from the order. Their former sales process began by meeting with the customer and discussing security needs, walking through the building, and taking notes. Afterward, the sales rep returns to the office and searches through product books and pricing (the average system contains 200 components and can cost a few hundred dollars to several million). Product books contain 12,000 items. Attempts to close the deal hit snags because jobs were incorrectly designed or the wrong item was chosen. After closing the deal, there was the job of posting and booking the paperwork, routing slips, certificate requests, alarm notification lists, authority dispatch lists, and sales worksheets. The forms require the customer's name and address to be written 12 times. The new system includes an expert system, floor plan graphics, account management system, fax, and E-mail. The system automatically poses questions and builds a bill of material, prepares a printed pricing proposal, and sets up contracts for the sales in less than 20 minutes. The system also handles leads. Security systems are rarely designed incorrectly now. Before, 80% of the alarm systems were designed incorrectly; that number is now below 5%. Wells Fargo decided its main goal was to find a way to eliminate the largest barrier to increased sales production—the time required by a sales rep to move from the assessment of a customer's needs to a written quote/proposal for that customer. Close ratios have risen from seven to eight per month, which generates an extra $8 million of revenue. They will now be able to hire people who are experts in selling and not engineering. Previously seven out of ten days of new employee training was done on product, with the last three on selling. Now this is reversed. The removal of administrative burden has lifted morale throughout the organization.[7]

❖ Val-Pak, a direct-marketing mail cooperative located in Largo, FL, produces customized Express Ads for local business. The company was experiencing a problem with poor close ratios on cold calls. Their solution was to develop a sales tool that runs on a laptop computer and allows the salesperson to customize an Express Ad in front of the customer. When the design is complete, the salesperson can print the ad. The system includes testimonials, movies, and information about Val-Pak. The sales rep also has access to the sales office when on the road. Close ratios on cold calls have gone from 10% to 30%.

■ Economic Evaluation

❖ The value associated with products and services can be tangible or intangible. This is particularly true when dealing with issues related to risk. Life-cycle costing of products can be equally tricky. It is not reasonable to expect a salesperson to conduct an effective presentation while making numerous calculations; thus, it is desirable to develop interactive presentations that use customer data and provide perspectives based on the customer's performance criteria.

❖ Nordstrom Valves, Inc., Sulphur Springs, TX, manufactures and sells to the oil and natural gas industries. Their product is considered the "Cadillac" of the industry. To illustrate the value of its products, Nordstrom implemented an interactive software program. The technology has proved useful to salespeople and to customers, who now have better information with which to select a valve. One of the keys of their sales success is to get the customer to specify Nordstrom valves upfront. However, with sales cycles as long as one year and prices that can be 15–25% higher, Nordstrom needed a better way to market. The program they developed compares the prices of Nordstrom's valves against competitors by factoring maintenance costs along the way. Salespeople now use the program to quickly demonstrate life-cycle cost analysis, ROI, and break-even analysis. The system also has a configuration capability of over 500 valves. Customers can input pressure and flow, and the system presents the results in a graphical and easily understandable format. Both the financial and configuration software can be left with the customer to configure products themselves.[8]

Forecasting

Projection of revenues and product mix typically falls into two processes; one is referred to as the annual plan, and the other is the forecast. The plan often represents an 18-month time horizon because the revenue figures are key to other planning activities. The forecast, on the other hand, has a 30- to 90-day time horizon. At a minimum, forecasting applications should handle the arithmetic functions and roll-up the numbers by territory. In addition, these applications may provide a historical perspective and provide graphical views of the current and projected numbers. These enhancements to a manual process may seem insignificant, but in the field, they can eliminate days from the process and weeks from delivering the final numbers. Also, with a reduction in manual numerical calculations, more attention can be given to the assumptions behind the numbers rather than the numbers themselves.

One very self-defeating characteristic of forecasting processes is to embark on a very time-consuming process, only to create numbers that are not used for decision making (marketing and manufacturing use their own numbers). When this is realized (it does not take long), the whole process takes on a cynical orientation. In general, the sales organization should provide input to the process to the degree that they possess unique insight regarding future purchase patterns. This suggests the salespeople should concentrate on changes in purchase behavior with regard to their largest customers (80/20 rule). When goal objectives are built into the account management application, salespeople can adjust their projections for the account as part of every call; in this way a dynamic forecast is created.

Another approach for forecasting is through the use of a proposal generator. A manufacturer of telephone switching gear installed a proposal generator application that tracked proposals as they were generated. Over time the company was able to extrapolate forecasts based on this database. The company developed a 97% availability level while employing a 30% lower inventory level than it had used in the past.

Communication

Communication is a key component of all aspects and phases of the sales process. It is listed under the Plan cycle to reinforce the importance of communicating and coordination strategy as it applies to overall tactics and specific account emphasis (e.g., national accounts).

Electronic mail lists can be set up with group codes so that messages pertaining to specific sub-groups within the sales organization will receive them (for example, all sales reps who have GE subsidiaries in their territories).

Hewlett Packard found that it could cut the time its sales reps spent in meetings from 13% to 7% by communicating with them electronically.[9]

Motivation

An important aspect of any sales planning process is to establish goals and the basis for commissions and bonuses. As outlined earlier, goals can be integrated into account management applications. This information can provide consistent reinforcement regarding progress toward goals.

More importantly, sales automation can facilitate the creation of bonus structures that are more closely tied to profitability. Historically, sales objectives have been tied to revenue, principally because the sales force was viewed as implementing marketing programs with little ability to impact price. Today's market conditions demand more flexibility to effectively deal with local market conditions. These pressures have required a shift in responsibility from marketing to sales. However, management tools are necessary to ensure sound and consistent decision making. Sales automation can provide decision-making and funds tracking applications that facilitate decentralization processes and empower the sales force to manage profit contribution.

Consumer goods companies have migrated to local marketing programs due to the ineffectiveness of mass media and the relative effectiveness of supporting marketing opportunities at the local level. Thus, if local management is to be held accountable for this funding, it needs to be based on a measure of profitability. Likewise, the medical supply industry has been rocked by managed care systems as they have emerged across the country. These demands have resulted in applications that track pricing and empower local management to execute sound strategies within each market. The result is bonuses based on profit contribution.

In a survey conducted by William M. Mercer, Inc., a New York sales consulting firm, only 10% of 450 companies said they link some portion of sales force compensation to customer satisfaction.[10] This is a curious statistic because other surveys have indicated that sales reps desire some of their compensation to be tied to customer satisfaction.

Channel Strategy

Sales automation can facilitate the coordination of channel strategy through electronic mail reports distribution and order entry. These applications with or without EDI can reduce administrative costs and accelerate cycle time, thereby improving the performance of the overall distribution and sales system.

A manufacturer of electrical components utilized a combination of agents and distributors to sell its products. Coordination, communication, and order entry all involved manual processes that resulted in redundant work being performed. The use of electronic mail, reports distribution, and order entry exercised enormous leverage to save significant levels of administrative effort while improving on-time delivery.

Call Targeting

An integral part of deployment, call targeting specifies priority contacts or accounts and call patterns (intensity of coverage). Historically, the pharmaceutical industry has provided a classical model for call targeting. Certain call patterns were found to be effective in gaining trial usage of new products by physicians. Since market share for new drugs is often established in the first three to six months in the marketplace, ultimate profitability is therefore determined by this introductory period. The obvious strategy is to execute the desired call pattern starting with the highest potential prescriber physicians and working back toward lower prescribers.

Since these call patterns demonstrate diminishing returns after a certain point, call targeting becomes a preeminent issue. This coverage relationship is captured in Figure 8.2.

With this type of leverage working in the marketplace, it is not difficult to understand why pharmaceutical companies were early adopters of the sales automation technology. It is interesting to note that one of the early entrants, Ciba-Geigy, sought the technology due to a need to merge the Ciba and Geigy sales forces. However, change is occurring in the pharmaceutical market in the form of managed care. In 1993, Hoescht Roussel, a pharmaceutical company located in Somerville, NJ, discovered that approximately 90% of physicians belong to at least one third-party managed care plan. Meanwhile, the sales force call targeting assumptions were built on the assumption that 65% of the physicians write 94% of the prescriptions. By targeting call strategy based on the leverage of managed care, the company was able to eliminate 125 sales reps while increasing total calls on high prescriber decision points.[11]

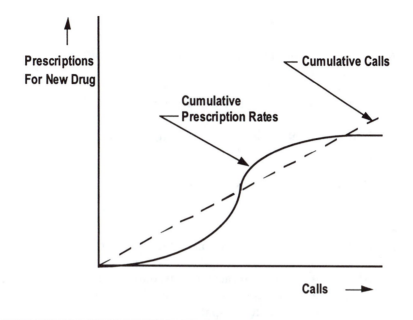

Figure 8.2   Relationship between call patterns and prescription rates.

Another example is a manufacturer of high-integrity valves, fittings, and flow control elements. They had voluminous information regarding 17,000 customers but no way to effectively share it with field sales. A sales force automation system provided, among other capabilities:

■ Sales history: trend analysis.

■ Potential of each customer and product line.

■ Forecasts based on short- and long-term projections.

The system shows salespeople where they have concentrated their calls, what customer needs are, and where the market potential is highest.

British Airways equipped U.S. salespeople with a system in 1993.[12] In the airline business, sales is often as much about education as persuasion. Reps are now better able to keep customers up to date. Before the new system, they had to spend time in the office to be knowledgeable. They now have ready access to essential account data no matter where they are:

■ 4,000 accounts each.

■ The types of business the client books with the airline (club seats, economy class, etc.).

■ Traffic patterns by origin and destination cities.

■ Information about how the travel agencies are selling the product.

■ Details on special deals or agreements.

Other applications include:

■ A tool to help to determine next call or call frequency.

■ Ability to generate contracts that customers can sign on the spot, thereby increasing call efficiency. Eventually they will get electronic signature capability.

■ The system looks for increases in air travel to destinations served by British Airways.

■ The system can often identify a customer's needs before the customer sees them.

■ The system enables sales reps to be proactive instead of reactive.

Sales reps are able to utilize their time more effectively by defining who they need to call, call preparation, and removing the need to physically go to the office for information. As the British Airways reps have experienced, sometimes the types of solutions are less important than the speed with which they can be put together.

Data General, a manufacturer of computers, reviewed overall field coverage and found that the 80/20 rule was operating, with coverage of their larger accounts getting a disproportionate amount of time. Rather than simply refining coverage criteria, field management started meeting with the smaller accounts to really define the type of services they felt they needed. The customers defined their needs as follows:

■ Reduced overall operating expenses for all information technology.

■ Improved price/performance.

■ Better information about new products in which they specifically might be interested.

■ Consistency of contact person (Data General was experiencing a high churn among field salespeople). The study indicated that customers welcomed a telephone sales approach for much higher volumes than expected, as long as service is there right away when needed.

The conclusion was that tele-sales could be combined with customer service to great effect. It captures the efficiency of tele-sales for the company and provides additional value to the customer. The core of the concept is to provide lower volume customers with access to a dedicated team that is responsible for their satisfaction. The results for the top 30 accounts, each with expected revenue of $25,000, actually averaged $196,000. Revenues have grown at a compound rate of 44%.[13]

Administration

Every field sales organization has some level of administrative tasks, such as call reporting, expense reports, vehicle reports, mail, maintenance of folders and binders, etc. In many cases the electronic version of these forms and applications takes about as much time as the original.

However, this tends to be the tip of the iceberg for most administrative processes. In most situations, there are mail costs, editing and correction costs, delays associated with correction, and the general waste of filing materials as performed by the sales rep. In addition, by eliminating paper, most sales reps will reclaim a closet, and the organization can save on the generation of forms. Thus, when the entire process cost and time performance are considered, there is no comparison between the electronic and paper processes.

Pre-Sale

Pre-sales activities represent a combination of qualifying and developing a sales strategy for each account. Qualification implies an assessment of whether the prospect is going to purchase within a relevant time frame, the likelihood that they will purchase from the salesperson, and the resource commitment required to "make it happen." Since the selling cycle is really one of making it easy to buy, pre-sales activity (Figure 8.3) is essential to optimizing sales results.

Lead Management

Lead management is as fundamental to sales productivity as is deployment. Timely follow-up on leads is often viewed by prospects as an indicator of overall performance; therefore, minimal turnaround time is desirable. From a sales management standpoint, it is desirable to "qualify" leads using lower cost, inside salespeople. The qualifying process needs to be effective in quickly winnowing the number of leads to a group that best represents success for the field sales rep as reflected in Figure 8.4.

It is highly desirable to integrate the qualification process with field automation. Leads can be integrated with account management (Figure 8.4). As the leads are qualified in the field, management can study the success rate and the reason for elimination. This analysis should further

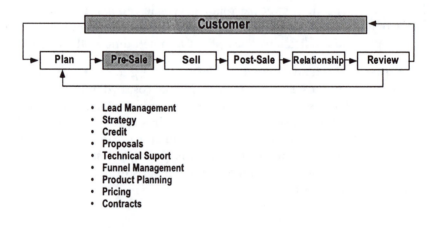

Figure 8.3   Elements of the pre-sale phase of the sales process.

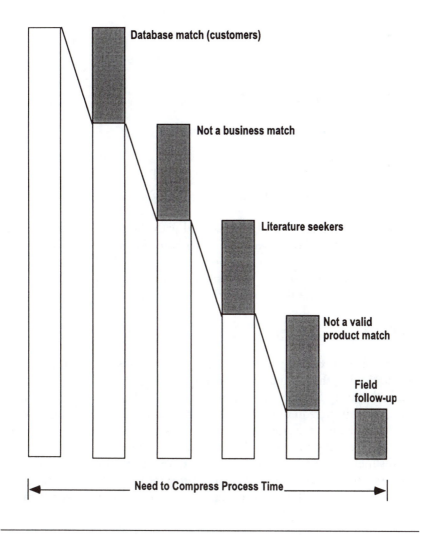

Figure 8.4 Elements of the qualification phase of the sales process.

sharpen the lead qualification process. Also, by linking the processes electronically, the time required to complete the process is reduced to a minimum. For example, Hewlett Packard, an early innovator in lead management, was able to reduce the turnaround from 14 weeks to 48 hours.

Lead management issues include:

■ Speed of processing

■ Solid qualification criteria

■ Lead database

■ Follow-through with literature

■ Evaluation of lead sources

■ Ability to track SIC codes

Sales automation must be integrated with the entire process so that the organizational investment can be maximized. Given the interest in the Internet, a web site can also be a source of leads. The qualification process would, in turn, provide insight regarding who is visiting the site and how to leverage that interface.

Strategy

In the context of the pre-sale phase, the rep must establish a strategy for positioning the company and selling to the prospect. For those companies that use a formalized sales process, the strategy follows this format; if not, the salesperson must adopt their own approach. The sales strategy should facilitate the customer's "buy cycle" and should drive the salesperson to prioritizing time and effort. Following a disciplined sales process has distinct advantages in terms of being able to better understand and interpret the qualification and closing processes. The table on page 139 illustrates mapping the buy cycle against the resources required to facilitate this cycle.

This table is obviously a simplification to illustrate the mapping process between buy and sell cycles. Sales automation can assist in this process by integrating the sales process into the territory/opportunity management software. This dramatically reduces the administrative aspects of these techniques while reinforcing the discipline of the sales process structure.

System Software Associates, Inc. of Chicago, IL, is a supplier of integrated manufacturing, logistics, and process planning software systems.

Buy Cycle	Resources					
	Tele-sales	Sales Rep	Manager	Tools	Skills	Programs
Unaware of opportunity	✓			Leads		
Openness to be informed	✓					
Motivated to seek solution		✓	✓			
Communicate need internally		✓				
Evaluate need and solutions		✓				Expert
Define solution criteria		✓		Analysis		
Evaluate solutions		✓				
Recommend solution		✓	✓			
Decision process		✓			Negotiate	
Commit to solution		✓				

The company's sales process involves 12- to 18-month sales cycles and requires salespeople to interface with executive level people within customer locations, including CFOs. Therefore, it was very important to the company to pursue the right business with the right level of contacts. The solution was to integrate the sales process into the opportunity management software. Not only did this reinforce the correct sales process, but it also reinforced the correct terminology, which is critical to interfacing with executive-level people.[14]

Credit

Credit approval is commonly incorporated in the pre-sale activity to secure the credit worthiness of the prospect. This process typically involves a form or a telephone call with specific prospect information. Sales automation can use an electronic form capability whereby the information can be sent to finance and the approval returned on the same form.

The advantage of the approach is that it does not tie up the salesperson or the credit person while the check is being made. The sales rep should be notified within 24 hours via an electronic link regarding approval. Another approach is to give sales reps access to Internet locations that provide similar information.

Proposals

The generation of quality proposals should be of utmost importance, yet proposal generation tends to vary considerably by individual. Sales automation provides a mechanism for customizing proposals while retaining a uniform level of quality and content.

In addition, the proposal generator can provide editing and configuration capabilities such that both pricing and description are complete and accurate. Since the application is on the sales rep's computer, proposals can be generated at the customer's office or on the road. For example, the Office Imaging Division of Eastman Kodak was able to reduce proposal generation time from three weeks to less than 20 minutes.[15]

Carl Zeiss, Inc. of Thornwood, NY, sells 54 different microscopes, each of which has 30–40 components. Spec sheets for these microscopes are 30–40 pages long. Prior to automation, bids, forms, and diagrams were completed by hand; then they were sent to one of six regional offices for input into the bid system. Once the computer generated the configuration and proposal, it was checked by a manager; minimum time was 24 hours. This system was obviously slow and resulted in sales reps being bogged down in paper, and despite the editing, mistakes still occurred. With their new sales automation system, bids are now available in minutes. The sales rep can sit down with a customer and generate a quote at the customer's site and print it out. Quotes get into the company's pipeline faster. Along with reduced turnaround time, the new system generates more accurate orders and provides a better basis for forecasting.[16]

Steel Case, Inc. of Grand Rapids, MI, is one of the largest sellers of office furniture in the world. Before automating their sales force, data was spread across many independent legacy systems. It would take weeks to provide a customer with a price because the salesperson would have to contact 18–22 people to get a pricing decision. These delays translated into lost business. The sales reps can now quote directly from their system and the difference is reflected in increased win ratios on high-value deals.[17]

Technical Support

Many field sales forces rely on either field-based or corporate technical resources to provide essential sales-related services (e.g., specify equipment) or answer in-depth questions. These technical resources are typically in short supply, so utilization is of prime concern.

Sales automation can facilitate scheduling and communication through electronic applications, while other applications such as sales tools and reference materials can help salespeople to be more self-sufficient. Configurator applications can take this process further by empowering the sales rep to respond to customer-based performance data with specific product recommendations.

Funnel Management

When the sales process involves significant lead times and closes represent major increments of revenue, a mechanism is required to ensure that the respective sales processes are moving along at an acceptable rate and that revenue requirements are going to be achieved. The classical response to this type of sales environment is to segment the sales process into phases; each phase has a distinct beginning and end point. For example, a selling process could consist of the following:

Phase I	Qualification
Phase II	Define requirements
Phase III	Submit proposal
Phase IV	Close

By monitoring the time required to move between phases, the sales resources required to make this happen, and the percentage of prospects that move from phase to phase, it is possible to know how many prospects need to be at each phase in order to generate the required number of

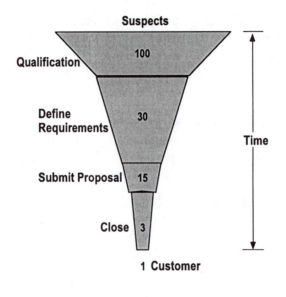

Figure 8.5   Conceptual model for funnel management.

closes to meet revenue requirements. Given the number of prospects, one can extrapolate the number of people required to make it happen! Figure 8.5 provides a graphical representation of these relationships.

Sales automation assists the process by assigning status levels within account profile screens. This type of information can feed a forecasting application that will automatically update projections. Thus, the system can reinforce the discipline of the process while reducing the administrative requirements of reporting status and revising forecasts.

For example, Storage Technologies, Louisville, CO, with $1 billion in annual revenue, was preparing to launch 14 new products when a survey discovered that salespeople spent the majority of their time performing administrative tasks and less than one-third of their time selling. Recognizing their inability to manage this level of new products with the current head count, they implemented a system that included E-mail, spreadsheets, word processing, proposal generation, and product pricing and configuration applications. At the end of the first year, salespeople were spending 45% of their time selling. Proposals can now be prepared in less than an hour. A typical sales cycle that previously took nine months and 50 calls was reduced by 25%. A new product feature can be announced immediately.

Pricing

Pricing applications can range from the distribution of price lists to configurators that accurately price complex product orders such as computer systems. Although pricing and price lists appear to be of nominal value on the surface, an effective system can have substantial impact on organizational administrative time and customer relations (value). A major chemical manufacturer has an entire department dedicated to managing contract and price changes. Every time a price change occurs, new pricing must be communicated to customers and adjustments made in the pricing system based on contractual terms. Unfortunately, without a contract database, the changes tend to lag events, resulting in debits and credits and delays in payment. The net of all this is a reduction in cash flow, wasted sales time, and angry customers.

Yellow Freight, a less-than-truckload shipping company located in Overland Park, IL, was plagued by duplicate effort and information, inconsistent sales practices, and poor communication. In developing their system, the guiding principle was to keep shipment information ahead of the physical flow of freight at all times. Before the system, salespeople would typically spend their first two hours of every day responding to customer inquiries and administrative duties. They had to do this at the terminal due to access to the mainframe system. This commitment represented double jeopardy because it wasted time, and morning is a prime time for selling. Before the installation of the system, reps had all the account information. Sales managers had to go to the rep to find out anything about the account. The new system includes E-mail, fax, mainframe connections, an account management module, and an application that lays out the products and services in a way that makes sense to the customer. Results from the install include more time in front of the customers (30%) and improved reporting consistency. The system gives sales staff critical information on customers, markets, and competition. It also allows sales reps and pricing staff to work together to formulate appropriate pricing strategies.[18]

Contracts

At the most rudimentary level, standard contract forms can be attached to applications that generate proposals. However, in this mode, all that is accomplished is the elimination of forms distribution in the field. The process of sending contract modifications to the legal department, etc., is common, along with its associated delays. An alternative is to study the pattern of modification to contracts and develop a modular approach so that field people can assemble contracts that cover 90% of the circumstances without the delays of legal review. This approach dramatically reduces response time and sales rep follow-up time and adds only modest increase in complication for the automation system.

Sell

The sales process should be oriented toward making it easy to buy! In this regard, the sales process offers enormous potential to add value for the customer. Unfortunately, most automation projects approach the process from a control standpoint rather than a close (value) perspective. Although there are elements of control in all of the applications discussed in this section, the focus will be on the value-added aspect of each application.

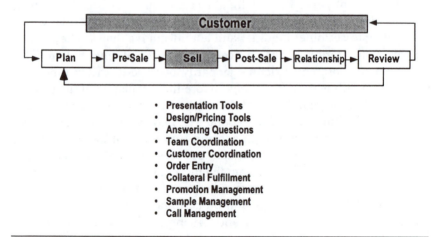

Figure 8.6   Elements of the sell phase of the sales process.

Presentation Tools

The nature of presentation tools was outlined in the discussion of Pre-Sale applications. This included software such as slide presentations and multimedia. Presentation tools are commonly used to position the company and its products/services. Presentation tools need to be flexible to respond to the nature of the prospect's business and the attendees of the presentation. The material needs to be current with the market and with product and service offerings. Once the tools are in place, the organization must keep the materials current; otherwise, there is a significant risk that the tools will not be used. For example, Pitney Bowes' initial applications included a capability to position sophisticated products on the notebook with simple presentation modules.[19]

Presentation tools can also be integrated with marketing encyclopedias. In this context, the tools can be pre-defined for product, industry, and certain competitors. This capability brings the power of marketing to the field in a seamless and effective manner.

Design/Pricing Tools

Design tools can be critically important to the sales process from a number of perspectives:

- Design tools represent a demonstrable way of differentiating the company and the sales rep.

- The salesperson is viewed as adding value.

- The more value sales reps add to the process, the more likely it is that they will be invited to participate in design meetings in the future. The earlier in the design phase participation begins, the more likely it is that the participating supplier will be chosen as the vendor of choice. In this position, margins become less of an issue.

- Design tools reduce the level of technical resources that are assigned to the field. These resources can be reassigned to development-oriented work.

■ The existence of a design tool can dramatically reduce cycle time because the customer can obtain specifications on the spot. Even when prototypes are involved, both the cost and turnaround time for the prototype are reduced.

Some examples of design tools include:

■ The use of CAD capabilities to produce sophisticated packaging designs in the paper industry. The design can be transmitted electronically to numerically controlled equipment that produces the sample.

■ Control systems can be designed according to customer application parameters. The system can specify component requirements and generate orders for prototype units.

■ The consumer goods industry uses software to generate recommended shelf layouts referred to as "planograms." Major manufacturers in each retail segment use these design services to position themselves as category leaders within the retail trade. Due to low margins in the industry, the way shelves are stocked can mean the difference between profit and loss. Reckitt & Colman, a manufacturer of household chemicals and specialty foods, located in Plano, TX, uses Apollo for space management and tracks scanner data for retailers. This allows the company to develop a planogram or design a store layout without going into the store. The system will analyze the movement of merchandise and competitors and propose what items should be added and discontinued and why.[20]

■ John Deere Power Systems Group builds and sells diesel engines for commercial uses. Given a design configurator, they can deliver a firm quote immediately. The application eliminates having to go back to the head office to check it. There are fewer errors and omissions. Information about bids that don't get the business is also captured and returned to marketing.

Answering Questions

The ability to provide correct and relevant answers to questions in the sell phase is critical to gaining credibility, meeting and exceeding expectations, and shrinking the duration of the sell phase of the process. In the description of reference materials in the planning phase of the sales cycle, applications were described that provide rapid access to reference material while eliminating the three-ring binders, etc. The advantages of this electronic capability are many, but one of the most important is to integrate answering questions when they are asked, rather than deferring them, which can lose continuity of a meeting or closing the business.

Another type of capability is related to tapping into the knowledge of the organization. Access to technical resources, sales management, and other sales reps can represent a decided competitive advantage. For example, using E-mail to gain an answer from engineering or R&D can reduce turnaround time by eliminating phone tag. Using electronic forms can help salespeople to get complete information from a prospect so that research people can answer the question the first time around or with minimum delay. Some organizations have effectively used bulletin board concepts as part of E-mail to post successes or selling situation needs where a salesperson is confronted with a situation or industry unfamiliar to the sales rep. The bulletin board concept can be very effective, but it requires a corporate culture where sharing information is reinforced and where there is commitment to supporting the sales effort. In general, quality questions beget quality answers in less time. The use of an electronic interface reduces communication waste while providing answers to the prospect faster than anyone else.

Pitney Bowes, the office and mail room equipment company, has 2,700 reps. Their applications include:

- An electronic brochure with pictures of company products that could be integrated into presentations.

- A disk-based version of a competitive blue book, a product comparison reference that had been delivered in three-ring binders.

- A rules-based application (configurator) to help salespeople write up orders without errors.[21]

Team Coordination

Team selling is a concept that has received higher visibility in recent years due to the complexity of products/services, the complexity of the buy decision process, and the prevalence of conglomerates that have many divisions. By its very nature, team selling infers combinations of the following:

- Sales/service team assigned to a major corporate facility.

- Multiple divisions of the supplier's company calling on the customer location.

- Coordination of various levels of field salespeople with corporate staff (consumer goods promotion activity).

- Salespeople geographically dispersed calling on divisions of the same corporate parent.

- Salespeople geographically dispersed that have distributors who supply divisions of the same corporate parent.

- A complex buy process that involves several functions and technical detail that exceeds the salesperson's ability to effectively handle. In this case, the salesperson may be coordinating internal resources, such as engineering, installation, marketing, finance, contracts, etc.

The constant within all of these situations is that the salesperson must coordinate efforts across the organization. If this is done entirely through phone contact and face-to-face meetings, it is not difficult to envision a time-consuming process for both salespeople and staff. Applications such as E-mail, scheduling, and account management reduce the need for direct contact. Electronic mail can be used for messages, schedules can be used to verify availability, and account management can be used to share profile and call information regarding the account. Thus, without voice contact, it is possible to share the needs and strategy for the account.

In August 1994, Wilson Learning Corporation and PenUltimate Software announced a partnership to create a sales automation software program that incorporates the lessons of Wilson Learning's target accounts selling program. The system is unique in that it steers salespeople through a company's sales cycle. One client, Ithaca Software, sells software that helps developers create graphical applications. They needed software that would share information with corporate staffers so that they could work together to close a deal, while the manger did efficient reporting and forecasting.[22]

The Gillette Company installed a pen-based system for its 250 reps in the retail merchandising group. Gillette is one of the top five manufacturers of health and beauty aids. The Merchandising Group merchandises products for the Grooming Division, which includes shaving and personal care products. Automation has given Gillette the ability to see marketplace conditions as no one else can. They chose pen-based units because reps work on their feet. In the retail business, out of stocks are important, so the system tracks these conditions closely. The reps also receive exception reports that tell them which items a store carries and when floor stands are up. Over the months, a statistical picture of product trends and store activity is created and downloaded. When the sales rep can show the store manager that he had out of stocks for the last four months, the rep can get action. Also helpful when sitting with a buyer, the account rep can tell him what occurred in the store as recently as two days ago. Reps get told about local advertising programs and new item codes. Gillette has a structured sales force including retail reps, key account reps, and district managers. One of the benefits of the system is that the managers are spending more time with their people. Key account people utilize data to give more interesting presentations (the only type of data collected is information that is of interest to the buyer).[23]

Some consumer goods companies are approaching promotion management with a project orientation. Tasks that are associated with the promotion and critical events such as ads, ability of stock, etc., represent dependencies that must be managed. Thus, one way to evaluate promotional performance is to note if the execution of the event had problems.

Telogy, Inc. is a Redwood Shores, CA, company that leases, rents, and refurbishes electronic testing and measuring equipment. Their sales department is divided into three distinct areas: an outside sales group calls on customers and establishes relationships with high potential prospects, inside sales provides customers who called in with configuration information, and 90-sales qualifies leads and tracks low potential prospects. Before the sales system was in place, integrated information could not be shared among the three sales groups. Invariably, bottlenecks occurred during sales process hand-offs. To get a price quote for a customer, an outside rep would call an inside rep, who would call the customer with the information. Many reps spent half their time gathering and re-keying data Customer contact information is now recorded in shared files, giving every salesperson the ability to manage a deal through the entire process. The company can now process an order in record time, including taking orders at 5 P.M., with guaranteed delivery of the equipment by 10 A.M. the next day. Telemarketing and direct mail campaigns are more effective because customer information can be quickly organized and sorted.[24] They have found a new sense of team effort. The new system automatically fills out a lease card, and leasing has jumped 20% since the automation process went into effect. Telogy has seen sales increase by 15% while cutting inventory by 10%.

Customer Coordination

The reality of the sales process is that in addition to coordinating internal resources, the sales rep must facilitate the prospect's internal buy process. In some situations, this is distinctly a sales advantage; however, it is always time consuming. At one level, this effort may be in the context of scheduling meetings or ensuring that their internal processes are working. In this form, account management tools, such as "to-do lists," will help.

A more complex form of facilitation occurs when the salesperson is confronted with a need to communicate "value" across functions. For example, medical instruments salespeople may need to convince physicians that their device has superior characteristics regarding absence of complications and effectiveness. A person in charge of a surgical suite may be interested in the time it takes to perform procedures, whereas an administrator may be interested in breadth of the product line to reduce the number of vendors. The CFO of the hospital may be interested in issues regarding inventory or outcome information. It would be wonderful from a sales standpoint if all these people talked to each other in value terms and if the supplier's product was superior in every regard, but this is seldom true. Thus, it is incumbent on salepeople to position their product in the correct context to each person in the decision process, and they must also communicate the other views or perspectives across the prospect's organization. Not only is this time consuming, but it is demanding from a knowledge and skill perspective. The salesperson may have no trouble talking with doctors but may have great trepidation about speaking with a CFO. The options are to get support from corporate staff, provide training, or provide sales tools that help the sales rep communicate these differences. Special applications can be developed that take these concepts and convert them to terms that each group will relate to. This reduces training time and the requisite skill level to do the job.

Within the consumer goods industry, some manufacturers are utilizing a strategy called "co-marketing" to more effectively leverage the investment in trade programs. Co-marketing is a partnership between retailers and manufacturers to increase both parties' revenue and profits. Rather than a specific set of activities, co-marketing involves the use of a range of marketing activities. The implications for sales are great. The salesperson must operate more as a business person rather than as a salesperson. Some organizations are retraining their people, while others are forming cross-functional teams composed of marketing, sales, and financial management. The purpose of the team is to make the manufacturing organization look more like that of the retailer. There is also a carry-over to how salespeople are evaluated. In the past, sales was evaluated on volume and revenue; now the measures are more likely to be profitable volume and profitable revenue.

Order Entry

Order entry applications are typically custom developed. Each organization's products, codes, and needs tend to be unique. Beyond simply performing the calculations associated with the process, order entry applications often have product stock levels downloaded at least every 24 hours. If availability of stock is a critical issue, wireless communication can be employed to verify availability and lock the available stock to the order. This adds value to the customer and can be a key capability for the salesperson. For example, in the apparel industry where seasonal and style-oriented goods have a short shelf life, back orders do not exist. Therefore, if a sales rep encounters a stock-out during the order entry process, he can work with the buyer to substitute sizes or colors to match the original order. Clearly, this is a key capability in this industry and has major revenue implications.

Order entry applications also tend to eliminate errors and omissions. This, in turn, eliminates the need for staff to review the orders and reduces overall cycle time.

Store door delivery represents an excellent example of several applications working in combination to support the sales rep. Anheuser-Busch has equipped its sales reps with applications to:

- Take orders for delivery within 24 hours.

- Track inventory and trace orders.

- Prepare a computer model to suggest order quantity.

- Check for special messages (e.g., the brewer might want a survey done on competitor prices or a special promotion tied with a sporting event).

Physician Sales and Service of Jacksonville, FL, is a distributor of medical supplies, equipment, and pharmaceuticals to doctors' offices. They recently installed a wireless order entry system. Order cycle time has been cut from two days to same day. Sales reps save eight hours per week. Business has increased by 255%. The salesperson does not have to call anyone to see if an item is available; overall, sales rep productivity has jumped 39%.[25]

Collateral Fulfillment

Collateral fulfillment pertains to situations where the salesperson does not have a full complement of materials that may be requested during the sales cycle. Examples of this type of process pertain to pharmaceuticals, medical products, chemicals, construction-related products, etc. In these situations, the sales rep must first identify what exists or otherwise articulate the need so that someone else from the supplier's staff can respond appropriately.

Sales automation provides a number of approaches to reduce administrative time, overall process time, and inventory-related costs. The solution often involves consolidation of literature to one location (domestic perspective) that is sometimes outsourced. All requests are directed to this one location; the requests are made electronically via the sales automation system using electronic forms or the account management application. Where there is considerable breadth to the available material or where the list is constantly being refreshed with new material, the system may offer a reference list with abstracts to ensure appropriate choices. Requests typically are sent within 24 hours of their receipt. The system can include a letter from the sales rep, thereby personalizing the response. The advantage of this approach is that inventory is housed in one location; therefore, it is easier to better manage the overall inventory. Response time for requests is often superior to that provided by sales reps or sales offices.

An emerging alternative to this approach is to set up a web site with direct access to relevant material. The site could be used for ordering or direct download of the material.

Promotion Management (Local Marketing)

Local marketing pertains to the discretionary use of discounts or other financial incentives to build the business at the local level. A common example of this situation is in the consumer goods industry where local funding is made available to support accounts in ways that are not possible through national programs. At the local level, both the sales rep and sales management must be concerned about using these funds wisely and to avoid overcommitment. Special applications can be developed to manage the use and availability of funds. Other applications can be used to facilitate planning with accounts so that investment will result in the desired market behavior. By integrating these capabilities within sales automation, corporate functions can monitor the use of the funds to ensure proper budgeting.

As an example, Kraft has assembled a centralized information system that collects and integrates data from three sources. The data it collects from individual stores break out consumer purchases by store, category, and product and indicate how buying behavior is affected by displays, price reductions, etc. A second database contains demographic and buying habit information (national). A third database is geo-demographic information by zip code. The trade marketing team sorts and integrates the information to supply sales teams with a repertoire of usable programs, products, value-added ideas, and selling tools appropriate for that store or area.

Sample Management

Sample management applications are common within the pharmaceutical industry due to a federal law that demands accountability for samples. These applications track inventory at the sales rep level and facilitate documenting transactions with doctors through electronic signature capture, adjustment of sample levels, and electronic updates to corporate. This approach eliminates a mountain of paperwork and speeds reconciliation of inventory at the sales rep level. This process also allows for faster evaluation of samples and prescription rate changes.

A similar need for inventory reconciliation occurs in the medical instruments industry, where consignment inventory is used as a mechanism for trial of new products. In this case, an inventory application facilitates accurate counts and provides input to the system to verify usage.

Other industries need to manage samples in the same context as leads. How are samples being used and how often do they lead to new business? For some industries where a sample is a real product, the cost of a sample is substantial. Use of samples can be integrated with account management or forms applications to track use of samples and its related business impact. Without this type of perspective, it would be hard to identify waste in terms of inappropriate targeting and identifying lower cost alternatives.

Call Management

Call management, more affectionately referred to as call reporting, has historically taken a preeminent position in the debate of sales automation. As was pointed out earlier, sales automation provides an opportunity to reinforce basic sales process disciplines while eliminating paper and administrative load. To the extent to which the discipline of the sales process can be linked to success in the field, this type of modeling makes perfect sense.

There are situations where call report content needs to be fairly extensive. For example, retail coverage within the consumer goods industry often involves capturing data regarding the condition of the store.

Gathering this type of data is key to effectively managing accounts at the headquarters level where the buyer knows more about throughput but lacks insight regarding store conditions that contribute to throughput. It is virtually impossible to gather timely retail data (other than pricing) through syndicated services; therefore, retail reps are a logical alternative source of data. In this regard, sales automation provides an effective method for recording conditions in a complete and accurate manner. Tools such as pen-based systems, bar coding, etc., offer mechanisms to quickly capture data and provide feedback to corporate and field sales at the end of the day.

Despite the hype and debate, it is difficult to question the need to treat a sales call as a meeting. Good management would suggest that keeping notes and items to follow up on are essential. If call reporting supports this orientation and helps the rep to keep track of to-do lists, sales automation serves a logical and useful purpose.

When one considers the disruptive implications of turnover in the field, call reporting and call history are invaluable tools for the new rep and, for that matter, the customer. Customers perceive as much waste as does the supplier's organization when turnover occurs.

Becton Dickinson AcuteCare Division of Franklin Lakes, NJ, supplies hospital operating rooms with gloves, scrubs, preps, and other disposable products. Their call management system includes an account record profile, call report, and E-mail. They have reported that sales reps spend less time searching for information and reporting on progress and more time in front of customers.[26]

Cahners Publishing, a Newton, MA, business magazine publisher, conducted a survey of its 4,000 advertisers and found that 41% of the customers were not called on during the previous twelve months. Only 16% of the sales reps made it a point to contact every one of their accounts at least once a year.[27] Clearly, this is a serious breach in call coverage, but it also raises the question of the underlying rationale of the sales reps. Are these other accounts worthy of the coverage and/or would they be better served with tele-sales coverage, wholesalers, or a web site?

Post-Sale

The post-sale period pertains to processes and events that occur after the order has been generated. This includes installation and post-installation service as appropriate.

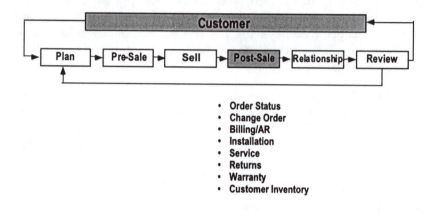

Figure 8.7   Elements of the post-sale phase of the sales process.

Order Status

Order status is essentially a report that provides an update of all the sales rep's orders in the system. Automation can essentially make these reports as current as necessary. Flags can be set to identify situations where the sales rep needs to intervene. Ideally, it would be desirable for the report to be one of simply verifying customer delivery dates; unfortunately, reality suggests that the sales rep be aware of deviations from promised delivery date. In this manner, the sales rep can be proactive in notifying the customer and offering alternatives. A nightmare for most sales reps is to be "ambushed" by the buyer concerning a missed delivery date.

Change Order

Change orders are related to order status. Order status alerts the sales rep of changes by the customer and otherwise allows the sales rep to be aware of the status of orders should the customer request changes.

Billing/AR

Billing and accounts receivable can be a major time sink for sales reps. Billing errors can be reduced by the use of configurators and order entry. These applications tend to reduce the number of mis-priced orders. Timely processing of contracts also reduces the window of opportunity for invoices to be released prior to a contract being logged into the system. Unfortunately, receivables often get directly impacted by invoicing accuracy problems. The net effect is an increase in receivables and significant troubleshooting for the sales rep. Thus, automation applications that reduce these events save staff and field sales time. Perhaps more importantly, customers are becoming more intolerant of invoicing errors and consider it an aspect of delivered quality.

Installation

Installation is also similar to order status in that it keeps the sales rep in the loop regarding installation schedules and any slippage.

Service

Post-installation service is often related to maintenance or supply of equipment. As such, a sales rep should receive regular reports regarding the status of the account. Similar to order status, there need to be flags that highlight problems before they become problems. Electronic reporting can keep the salesperson up to date, but in some industries, the salesperson becomes directly involved in the service issue.

Nalco Chemical, of Naperville, IL, employs 2,000 salespeople worldwide. Senior management wanted to see increases in customer satisfaction as well as ease and efficiency for the sales staff. Their project includes some 30 applications that range from answers to "what-if" questions to performing on-site statistical process control and return on investment calculations. Nalco experienced a $14 million increase in sales, which the company attributes largely to customer response to the new applications. The applications have improved Nalco's ability to retain their business. Unlike vendors of commodity chemicals, Nalco emphasizes services and acts essentially as an outsourcer of chemical services from delivery to disposal. Future plans include linking the computers to process control devices at customer sites. These links will deliver an automatic warning call to Nalco sales staff should something go wrong at a customer site.[28]

Returns

Most companies would like to think of themselves as being easy to do business with, yet when return material is at issue, the red tape tends to get very thick. One solution is to empower the sales rep to make the decision. Sales automation can expedite the process by providing a mechanism to secure a return material number and complete the details electronically to satisfy the receiving function. If a forms application is involved, it should be possible to monitor the number of these shipments that are in the system and manage the disposition process inside the supplier's organization. These mechanisms result in rapid action and resolution by the supplier. This data can be entered into a database for analysis of patterns within product, industry, customer, or sales rep.

Warranty and Contracts

Contract information can be a key sales tool for industries that operate on a contract basis, particularly the service industry. This type of information can be integrated into account management so that sales reps are consistently informed regarding renewals within their accounts, as well as within competitive accounts.

Customer Inventory

Monitoring customer inventory can be an integral task of sales reps within certain industries. For example, consumer goods sales reps at the retail level assess inventory to ascertain movement or otherwise make recommendations regarding suggested orders. This is particularly true of store door delivery people.

Another example of this requirement is hospital supply companies. Due to the high cost of inventory, hospitals are contracting with manufacturers and distributors to basically manage the inventory in specific areas, for example sutures. To accommodate these capabilities within reasonable call frequencies, the sales reps are equipped with pen-based systems that facilitate a quick inventory count by line item. One rationale for using the sales rep for this process is that it projects value added while providing a natural setting for discussion of usage and preferences.

Relationship Building

Research conducted by Learning International had identified twenty practices that characterize successful long-term customer relationships. Salespeople contribute to the development of this relationship when they:[29]

■ Build interpersonal trust.

■ Create and sustain a positive image of the sales organization.

■ Inspire respect for the company.

■ Demonstrate concern for their customers' long-term as well as immediate interests.

■ Identify ways to strengthen the quality of their business relationships.

■ Help the customer meet needs within his or her organization.

■ Resolve issues openly and honestly.

■ Deliver on promises.

According to a 1985 TARP study, it is five times more expensive to get a new customer than it is to keep an existing one.[30] Moreover, it is estimated that 65% of all business comes from existing customers.[31] Therefore, the post-sale relationship-building processes are key to future profitability and sales performance (Figure 8.8).

Reports Distribution

The quality and timeliness of reports are key to providing sales reps with insight regarding the performance of the account. Sales automation projects should provide a decision-oriented database (see Chapter 6) to support the analysis of account performance. In addition to these reports being useful for analysis, the reports can also serve as a warning sign that

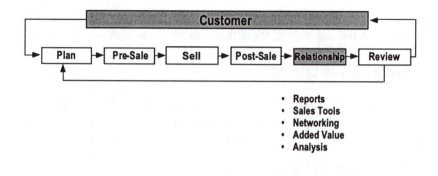

Figure 8.8 Elements of the relationship-building phase of the sales process.

coverage is not adequate. For example, sales reps sometimes use shipment reports as an indicator of the "health" of their B- and C-level accounts. If volume patterns change, it is a signal that attention is required.

Sales automation, at a minimum, should provide a mechanism to deliver pre-formatted reports to the field. In most situations, this step alone will take five to eight days off the delivery of reports via regular mail.

Quaker Oats built a PC-based decision support tool named "Mikey" that lets sales offices access and query corporate marketing databases. A sales office can use modules for business review reporting, market planning, ad-hoc reporting, and general information.

Sales Tools, Added Value, and Networking

Most organizations totally neglect the need to provide tools for the sales rep to use in the relationship-building aspect of account development. Influence is built through networking within organizations and adding value. Sales tools such as those presented in the sales and pre-sales discussion are appropriate for this phase; however, applications alone are not going to make it happen. The supplier organization needs to help the salespeople with content. Material regarding the customer's industry, trends in the supplier's industry, and the direction of the supplier's organization are vital communication vehicles. In this regard, the sales and marketing organizations must be dedicated to delivering quality material to facilitate this process. The sales rep must use these tools along with an entrepreneurial spirit to understand the needs of the organization and tailor the response to meet the needs.

For example, in the medical instruments and pharmaceutical industry, it is not uncommon for salespeople to present training programs to hospital staff. These presentations provide insight into developments in areas of specialty and provide accredited instruction that hospital professionals must have to retain their certification.

Analysis

Analysis should embrace each major account, as well as the territory at large. Some of the indicators may be built into territory management (e.g., how close is planned coverage to actual coverage? Is time commitment commensurate with the value of each account? What is the profit contribution of this account and the territory at large? How does it compare with similar accounts and territories?). Based on this and other analysis, sales reps need to determine how to strengthen their position within the account. Sales automation can facilitate this process by providing standard reports and providing more open-ended analytical capabilities to better understand opportunities and threats.

Review

Business reviews are probably one of the most overlooked strategic weapons in the corporate arsenal. A properly attended and configured business review can reveal a great deal regarding a customer's attitudes, direction, and priorities. One of the problems is that business reviews are approached as though they are a "drill" rather than a key strategic meeting. Part of the reason for this approach is the tendency to view all accounts on an equal basis as opposed to recognizing both size and innovative leadership. Senior management must be attuned to these opportunities to thank customers for the business but also gain a glimpse of the customers' perspective regarding their markets, how they compete in those markets, and what their priorities are.

From a sales rep standpoint, a review (Figure 8.9) is an opportunity to thank customers for their business and also to present a value presentation to the customer. This presentation is sometimes referred to as "Proof of Value" (POV). A POV presentation reinforces the ways that the

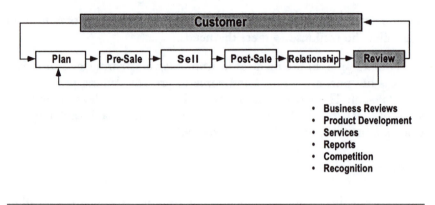

Figure 8.9   Elements of the review phase of the sales process.

supplier provides value to the customer. The mere orientation of the presentation helps to focus the sales rep and, hopefully, the organization at large on this important issue. A proactive approach of this type helps to form the concept of value consistent with the way the supplier is positioning it. Without such a presentation, the supplier is depending on the customer to perceive the delivered value; indeed, that is a dangerous assumption.

Business Reviews

Business reviews should be forward looking in purpose. Though the presentation starts with a review of the business from a historical basis, it is only relevant to the extent that it speaks to the future. Thus, the business review must be dedicated to future plans. Sales automation can facilitate this process in a number of ways:

■ Reports distribution can be used to provide appropriately formatted reports in a timely fashion.

■ Marketing and sales should provide materials that address the future of the company and the market. Presentation tools and multimedia can be used to present this material in a professional manner.

■ Account management screens can be used to capture account direction and goals.

■ Business reviews may be documented with a few basic questions for further marketing analysis. Electronic forms or account management may be used for such an application.

It cannot be stressed enough that the business review is a key event to check assumptions. For example, the marketing department for a Fortune 100 company "knew for sure" that customers were buying a certain component on the basis of price and technology. A subsequent survey of customers later demonstrated that 90% of the customers were buying on the basis of delivery and the availability of technical design assistance. When this was known, the company revamped the entire sales and sales support function to deliver against this criterion.[32]

Product/Services Development

Much has been written about customer surveys not being reliable as an input to product/service development, but this assumes that questions are asked relative to preferences. If the business review concentrates on how the customer competes today and intends to compete in the future, this opens the door regarding needs and priorities. The interpretation of this input can lead to new product and service features that neither party would have considered if the focus was on the existing offerings.

According to an article entitled "Customer Intimacy and Other Value Disciplines," Michael Treacy and Fred Wiersema have determined that companies that have taken leadership positions in their industries in the last decade typically have done so by narrowing their business focus, not broadening it.[33] These companies have focused on delivering superior value in line with one of three value disciplines.

■ **Operational Excellence**

❖ Providing customers with reliable products or services at competitive prices, delivered with minimal difficulty or inconvenience. These companies seek ways to minimize overhead costs and intermediate production steps, reduce transaction steps and other friction costs, and optimize business processes across functional and organizational boundaries. For example, with Dell Computers, PC buyers do not have to sacrifice quality or state-of-the-art technology to buy personal computers easily and inexpensively. General Electric's virtual inventory, a computer-based logistics system, allows stores to operate as though they had hundreds of items in stock. Meanwhile, GE gets half the dealers' business and saves about 12% of distribution and marketing costs. In addition, most other companies cannot tell if a retailer is ordering for inventory or for a customer; this is key to forecasting and understanding demand.

■ Product Leadership

❖ These companies offer leading-edge products and services that consistently enhance the customer's use or application of the product. They strive to produce a continuous stream of state-of-the-art products and services. To accomplish this innovative stream, they must be creative, which means recognizing and embracing ideas that usually originate outside the company. They commercialize their ideas quickly. Business and management processes have to be engineered for speed. Such companies relentlessly pursue new solutions to the problems that their own product or service just solved (e.g., J&J's quick commercialization of disposable contact lenses).

■ Customer Intimacy

❖ These companies are experts at segmenting and targeting markets precisely and then tailoring offerings to match exactly those niches. They tailor and shape products and services to fit an increasingly fine definition of the customer. Their strategy is to build customer loyalty for the long term. Corporate examples of this include Staples, Ciba-Geigy, Kraft, and Frito-Lay. Kraft has created the capacity to tailor its advertising, merchandising, and operations in a single store to those store's customers.

❖ The leadership companies become champions in one of these areas while meeting industry standards in the other two. It is hard to catch up to the leaders because they have aligned their entire operating model culture, business processes, management systems, and computer platforms to serve one value discipline.

Reports

Feedback from the business reviews should be formalized but consistent with the strategic significance of the accounts involved. More detail should be derived from high-leverage accounts. Sales automation can effectively move this data into a database environment for analysis. The technology helps to reduce administrative load while maintaining data integrity and minimizing acquisition time.

Competition

Business reviews may reveal directional plans of competitors. Assuming the existence of a competitive database, such information, particularly if it is reinforced at several reviews, can provide valuable competitive insight.

Recognition

The review time frame should also be an excellent opportunity to recognize top performance by salespeople. Recognition is often used as an incentive above and beyond bonus and commissions. The significance of sales automation is that the type of data and capabilities of the system provide new opportunities to recognize salespeople for performing like business people.

A pilot study conducted by Pitney Bowes demonstrated sales rep productivity gains of 30% and a significant improvement in customer satisfaction ratings.

Conclusions

This chapter has identified a wide range of applications and processes. The breadth of these applications reinforces the need to be able to utilize "best-of-breed" applications to assemble the ultimate system. Likewise, the scope of the applications and the processes reinforces the need to phase in applications and, in some cases, the scope of applications over time. As the sales organization becomes more sophisticated and disciplined, it is possible to build on systems to more completely leverage the available investment.

The remainder of the book will concentrate on the issues of evaluation and implementation. The potential impact of various applications will be revisited in Chapter 12.

Endnotes

1. Gilbert A. Churchhill, Jr., Niel M. Ford, and Orville C. Walker, Jr. *Sales Force Management* (Boston: Irwin, 1993), 232.

2. Melissa Campanelli, "Reshuffling the Deck," *Sales & Marketing Management,* June 1994, 83–90.

3. Alan R. Earls, "Brave New World," *CIO,* June 1, 1995, 86.

4. Weld F. Royal, "On-Line at The Prudential," *Sales & Marketing Management,* June 1994, 42.

5. Jeffrey Young, "Can Computers Really Boost Sales?" *Forbes,* August 28, 1995, 85–86.

6. Ibid., 88.

7. Melissa Campanelli, "Sound the Alarm," *Sales & Marketing Management,* December (Part 2) 1994, 20–25.

8. Megan Santosus, "New Value Systems," *CIO,* October 1, 1994, 80.

9. Allan J. Magrath, *Zero-Defect Marketing* (New York: American Management Association, 1993), 43–44.

10. Andy Cohen, "Right on Target," *Sales & Marketing Management,* December 1994, 59.

11. Campanelli, "Reshuffling the Deck," 83–90.

12. Tony Seideman, "A British Revolution," *Sales & Marketing Management,* August 1994, 115.

13. Domenic Troiano and Michael Troianl, "Profile: Data General's High Technology Customers Benefit from Telesales," *Telemarketing,* November 1994, 38–44.

14. "Training," *Sales & Marketing Management,* February 1995, 38.

15. Mellissa Campanelli and Thayer C. Taylor, "Meeting of the Minds," *Sales & Marketing Management*, December 1993, 83.

16. Thayer C. Taylor, "Making More Time to Sell," *Sales & Marketing Management*, May 1994, 40–41.

17. Stephen Mills, "Hard Sell," *CIO*, October 1, 1995, 112.

18. Mike Fillon, "Keep on Trucking Yellow," *Sales & Marketing Management*, June (Part 2) 1995, 17–19.

19. Campanelli and Taylor, "Meeting of the Minds," 83.

20. Ginger Trumfio, "For the Love of a Laptop," *Sales & Marketing Management*, March (Part 2) 1995, 31–34.

21. Jeffrey Young, "Can Computers Really Boost Sales?" 92.

22. Malcolm Fleschner, "Training that Lasts," *Personal Selling Power*, March 1995, 32–33.

23. Tony Seideman, "On the Cutting Edge," *Sales & Marketing Management*, June (Part 2) 1994, 18–23.

24. Megan Santosus, "Pursuing the Perfect Pitch," *CIO*, June 1, 1994, 33–34.

25. Thayer C. Taylor, "Sales Automation Cuts the Cord," *Sales & Marketing Management*, July 1995, 110–115.

26. Andy Cohen, "A New Surgical Tool," *Sales & Marketing Management*, September 1994, 49–50.

27. Thayer C. Taylor, "SFA: The Newest Orthodoxy," *Sales & Marketing Management*, February 1993, 96.

28. Jeff Moad, "IS Satisfies the Customer," *Datamation*, October 1, 1993, 79.

29. Stephen G. Haines and Katie McCoy, *Sustaining High Performance* (Delray Beach, FL: St. Lucie Press, 1995), 69–90.

30. William C. Johnson and Richard J. Chvala, *Total Quality in Marketing* (Delray Beach, FL: St. Lucie Press, 1996), 4.

31. Ibid.

32. C. Welch and P. Geissler, "Measuring the Total Quality of the Sales Function," *National Productivity Review*, Autumn, 517–31.

33. Michael Treacy and Fred Wiersema, "Customer Intimacy and Other Value Disciplines," *Harvard Business Review,* January-February 1993, 84–93.

CHAPTER 9

SALES MANAGEMENT: THE FORGOTTEN ELEMENT

Historical View of Management

As was described in the beginning of this book, the evolution of the technology that is available today had its roots in command and control thinking. Therefore, vendor presentations historically included some version of a three-tiered model for system usage, as indicated in Figure 9.1.

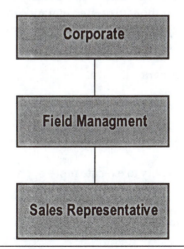

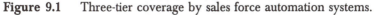

Figure 9.1 Three-tier coverage by sales force automation systems.

The disconnect with the model is the assumption that the needs of each level are basically fed by the sales rep (control orientation). Given the limitations of systems in the beginning of the industry and the pure functional structure of user organizations, this was a reasonable accommodation. However, business needs and available technology have changed in ways that suggest field management needs to consider issues beyond the sphere of the sales rep. The time has come for systems to address the needs of sales managers in the context of their roles and responsibilities.

The Forces of Change

The sales organization is one of the most productive and, at the same time, most expensive functions within most corporations. In the growth period of 1950–1980, it was sufficient to maintain parity between revenue and cost, but in today's market conditions, sales must be able to articulate a strong cost/benefit rationale for all elements of expense.

Corporate downsizing and cost reduction have reduced sales staff at the headquarters and field levels. Many organizations have eliminated sales offices. In addition, restructuring has eliminated layers of management or otherwise expanded the span of control of field management. Similarly, complementary functions (i.e., human resources, training, and marketing) have also reduced head count. The result of these changes is an expansion of field management responsibility and a blurring of functional responsibilities. At the same time, demands in the marketplace give cause for increased expectations regarding response time and effectiveness. All of these pressure points impact the sales manager as follows:

- Larger span of control.

- Less administrative support in the field.

- Fewer support resources available at headquarters.

- Added responsibility to execute more open-ended programs/ strategies.

- Expanded responsibility for profitability.

■ More responsibility for training sales reps based on fewer resources and less training done at headquarters.

■ Increased use of multiple distribution channels.

Clearly, without some type of systems support, this is an untenable situation. The remainder of this chapter will address these changes in greater detail and comment on appropriate applications of technology.

The Changing Role

It is often easier to understand and project change when it can be viewed as a continuum. The following chart provides two views of field sales management:

Category	Pre-1980s	1990s
Sales force composition	Direct sales force Distributors	Direct sales force Tele-sales Distributors Wholesalers VARS Electronic (EDI, the Net)
Types of positions	Territory sales reps District or area managers Regional managers	Territory sales reps Key account reps National account managers Sales support reps Customer service reps Telemrkt./sales reps District managers Regional managers Industry specialists
Marketing approach	Mass marketing techniques targeting one type of customer	Market segmentation techniques targeting several customer niches
Management style	Direct and control	Lead and coach
Performance expectations	Increase sales volume, meet budget levels, and minimize turnover	Increase sales volume in strategic markets, strategic products Increase margin contribution Decrease cost of sales Attract top sales performers Maximize customer satisfaction

Even with this simplified chart, it is easy to note the increasing complexity of the sales organization and the multifaceted performance criteria. Today's sales management force must achieve far more complex priorities and goals while simultaneously working with a more diversified set of resources.

Customer Expectations

As indicated in Chapter 8, the sales process needs to mirror the "buy process" in order to make the purchase process easy. This means that companies will have to place managers and salespeople in the field with skills and knowledge that match those found and used by their customers' procurement teams. According to a 1993 Center for Advanced Purchasing Studies (CAPS) report, these capabilities can be described by the following characteristics:[1]

Skills and Abilities	Knowledge Areas
1. Interpersonal communication	1. Total quality management
2. Customer focus	2. Cost of poor quality
3. Ability to make decisions	3. Supplier relations
4. Negotiation skills	4. Analysis of suppliers
5. Analytical skills	5. Lowest total cost
6. Management of change	6. Price/cost analysis
7. Conflict resolution	7. Source development
8. Problem solving	8. Quality assurance
9. Influence and persuasion	9. Supply chain management
10. Computer literacy	10. Competitive market analysis

This list represents a significant challenge to the traditional view of the sales process because virtually all of these characteristics are related to facilitating **the customer's buy cycle**. The challenge for the supplier is to hire people with this aptitude and then provide them with the training and experience to become proficient at these capabilities. As will be discussed in Chapter 10, it is questionable whether training alone can provide salespeople and management with sufficient insight in some of these areas to move from awareness to understanding. For example, the implications of quality and cost can be taught, but they are just concepts until they are applied. Therefore, the traditional career path for sales management may need to be reexamined.

From a sales rep behavior and attitude standpoint, customers are looking for a longer term perspective. This translates into the following type of transition:

Traditional Characteristics	Desired Characteristics
Knows internal contacts	Knows the whole business
Knows the product	Knows the customer's business
Makes every sale unique	Follows a standard process, that is modified to meet the customer's needs
Works hard to look good	Makes the organization look good
Is monetarily motivated	Is motivated by performance
Gets new customers	Keeps proven customers
Job hops	Is committed to the company
Sells the product	Sells solutions
Finds ways to beat the system	Works to change the system
Sells overtly	Provides easy buying

Thus, the sales manager must transition sales resources to meet the changing expectations of the customer while continuing to meet increased performance demands. This type of reinforcement is possible when the manager is with the reps, but, clearly, other types of reinforcement are necessary.

In a joint survey conducted by *Sales & Marketing Management* and Personnel Corporation of America, 76% of participants rated retaining existing accounts as very important; only 63% rated themselves as very effective at doing it. Similarly, while gaining share within existing accounts was rated as important by 68% of respondents, only 39% saw themselves as very effective at accomplishing that goal.[2] These statistics reflect either a lack of understanding regarding value, the buy cycle, and customer priorities or a perceived inability to make it happen. It is clear that the sales community is not equipped for today's environment, much less the demands of the future.

Leadership and Training of Subordinates

In today's evolving environment, effective sales managers must perform four distinct roles:

1. **Strategist**: A sales manager's role is to translate the company's strategy from a boardroom vision to an everyday reality, add value for customers beyond that provided by the products and services, create competitive differentiation, and contribute to the company's profitability.

2. **Communicator**: The sales manager must be able to convert the needs of the organization into actions and programs that people will relate to and respond to.

3. **Coach**: The sales manager gains influence through collaboration and setting mutually agreed goals, not by telling salespeople what to do. This type of mentoring takes time and patience for the manager. It is easier and faster to direct and instruct, but the implications on performance are enormous.

4. **Decision maker**: The sales manager must be able to determine if his strategy is working and make a myriad of market-level decisions "on the fly." The field manager is confronted with the delicate balance of delegating decisions to reps so as not to create a bottleneck.

In addition to coaching skills, many training organizations are seeing a distinct shift for field managers to also be trainers.[3] Pete Bonner, senior vice president of the American Society for Training and Development, noted that there are fewer internal sales trainers. Dartnell, a sales training company based in Chicago, IL, agrees that companies are no longer using the designation "trainers"; the function seems to be pushed to the manager level. Learning International, a sales training company, found that ten years ago, more than 60% of its customers were training professionals, with the rest being sales and marketing executives; now the numbers are reversed. Companies are hiring managers who have training background and asking existing managers to be coaches and mentors to their staffs. Its important to find out what salespeople want before you plunge into sales training. Having sales managers oversee sales training programs can be one of the more positive aspects of a company's downsizing or restructuring program.

In a leadership study of more than 25,000 employees (2,000 salespeople), 69% of employee job satisfaction was found to stem from the following leadership skills of managers:[4]

■ The ability to provide employees with a sense of mission.

■ The ability to create a work environment where people can stretch their talents but also know they will be able to complete projects.

■ The ability to provide feedback on what people need to improve on so they don't have to guess.

■ The ability to offer recognition and rewards in an appropriate way so that individual salespeople are recognized, as well as the team as a whole.

■ The ability to help and support employees in developing their talents and careers.

The net of this discussion is that the human element of what the sales manager does in the field is absolutely critical to motivation and turnover in the field. Although technology is powerful, having proper management support is key to an effective field organization. The objective then must be to provide sales management with the hard tools to organize the work and manage the business so that there is sufficient time for the manager to correctly conduct the soft aspects of the job with maximum effect.

Senior Management Support

The results of a Korn-Ferry International study of 1,500 executives from 20 countries predict changes expected in characteristics of managers by the year 2000 and are summarized below:[5]

	1988	2000	Change
Readily reassigns/terminates individuals	34	71	+37
Frequently communicates with customers	41	78	+37
Frequently communicates with employees	59	89	+30
Promotes management training and development	58	85	+27
Conveys strong vision of the future	75	98	+23
Rewards loyalty and length of service	48	44	−4
Personally makes all major decisions	39	21	−18

To the extent to which these characteristics match the ones of senior management, they will be welcomed by sales management. In essence, these shifts emphasize a sense of accountability to the customer and a desire to invest in people. There is an implication that senior management will provide an effective sense of direction for the organization and will be willing to take action when non-performance occurs. These shifts are all consistent with the needs of sales management; the challenge, however, will be to develop a strategy to provide the requisite training and tools to get the job done.

Marketing

In an article by Robert Blattberg and John Deighton, the authors provide a comparative perspective regarding the move from mass marketing to interactive marketing.[6] Although this analysis is consumer-goods oriented, it does provide a sense of the magnitude of the changes in marketing approach and the impact on the sales function.

	Mass Marketing	Interactive Marketing
Segmentation	Marketers measure the demographic and psychographic profiles of current customers or likely converts. They group together individuals with smaller profiles and treat them as if they were identical.	Marketers use actual behavior to identify customers and prospects and statistical models to assess the value of each address. Each customer can receive a customized offering.
Advertising	Communications are designed for the mean of the target group.	Advertising can use information on the individual customer. Computer-driven magazine binding allows selective insertion of print advertising.
Promotion	Promotion offers are broadcast using tools such as free-standing newspaper inserts or are mailed indiscriminately to homes defined by geo-demographics.	Promotions tailored to individual's past behavior are based on payout anticipated from promoting to that consumer.
Pricing	Price discrimination has to depend on customer self-selection.	Price discrimination exploits knowledge of the individual's price sensitivity and is delivered to that individual alone.
Sales Management	Customer data tends to reside with the salespeople who use it at their discretion to achieve their own goals.	Sales management has access to customer files and can use them to achieve organizational goals. It can implement targeted calling programs which can be updated by the use of lead generation and tracking systems.
Distribution Channels	The organization depends on intermediaries and direct selling from a sales force to reach customers. The customer tends to be owned by the channel intermediary or sales force.	The firm has direct links to the customer. When it uses intermediaries, it can jointly manage leads and customer relationships. Other elements of the marketing

	Mass Marketing	Interactive Marketing
		mix (promotion, advertising) can be timed to help move the customer through the decision process toward the purchase.
New Products	R&D is driven by the firm's technology and production systems.	The company offers new products and services on the basis of their affinity with the customer's. Marketers tend to serve their customer's base by selling outsourced products on behalf of third parties.
Monitoring	Market share sales and profit are the critical monitoring tools. Reviews tend to be periodic, usually annual.	Traditional measures are supplemented by measures of success in retaining customers and margin over cost of acquiring new customers. The value of the customer base is monitored with lifetime value calcula-tions. Monitoring tends to be continuous rather than periodic.

The major thrust of this chart is the need to target the customer and, to the degree possible, be interactive with that customer in delivering value. This has implications for sales and marketing, particularly with respect to the shifting of responsibility. The classic functional definition for marketing includes product management, sales management, and customer service. Figure 9.2 provides a sense of how the responsibilities of each function are being shared. Part of the reason for this is reduction in staff, but another component is the realization that these processes are horizontal in nature and, therefore, share responsibility in lower costs and shorter cycle times.

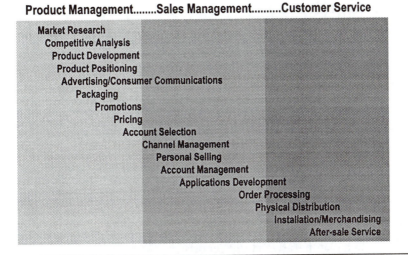

Product Management........Sales Management.........Customer Service

Market Research
Competitive Analysis
Product Development
Product Positioning
Advertising/Consumer Communications
Packaging
Promotions
Pricing
Account Selection
Channel Management
Personal Selling
Account Management
Applications Development
Order Processing
Physical Distribution
Installation/Merchandising
After-sale Service

Figure 9.2   The blurring of functions between marketing, sales, and customer service.

Technology Needs

It is apparent from the emerging trends in organizational structure and marketplace demands that the sales manager must transition to a role more analogous to a general manager. Further, the sales manager must accomplish these responsibilities with minimal staff assistance. This is a significant challenge!

The sales force automation applications discussed thus far provide some assistance in terms of communication and administration (mail and forms). The availability of reference materials and interactive training will also help the manager in terms of avoiding time out of the field and tailoring training to specific sales rep needs. In addition, account management applications can be customized to help integrate strategies, objectives, and tactics, thereby reinforcing actions the manager might otherwise have to reinforce in person. The real outstanding issues are a (1) database that is consistent in content with the types of planning and decision making that field sales management must make and (2) a reporting capability that facilitates seeing the "big picture" and evaluating cause and effect. This data system must be capable of the following:

1. Baseline Planning

- How can resources be used to provide the best possible performance?
- What needs to be done?
- What is the competition doing and what direction are they moving in?
- Where is the organization at this point?

2. Monitoring Reports

- Field reports
- Customer survey reports
- Comparative study reports
- Lost customer reports
- Competitive analysis
- Complaint analysis

3. Trend Analysis

- ROI analysis
- Profitability
- Organizational performance
- Organizational effectiveness
- Market share
- Changing customer perspectives

4. Optimization Tools

- Deployment
- Use of local marketing resources
- Analysis of product mix
- Pricing strategies

In general, field management must have analytical tools to understand current position and the need for change and planning tools that facilitate setting direction, establishing goals and monitoring progress, and "big dial" reporting. With the breadth of responsibilities, field management must be able to rely on major indicators to identify a need for action; this reporting may come in the form of trend reports or exception reports, but they must clearly flag problem areas.

From a technology perspective, the answer to these needs must be embedded in three basic applications:

- A planning model that helps field management to set direction, allocate resources, and establish accountability throughout the organization so that everyone is pulling in the same direction (alignment).

- Database development. Consistent with the concept of a data warehouse, sales management must have ready access to data that may reside in a number of locations within the organization to facilitate business-oriented decisions.

- Reporting and decision support tools are necessary to evaluate what's working and where problems exist.

The challenge for the sales automation industry is to make this integration seamless and user friendly enough for a manager to learn and effectively utilize.

Training Needs and Career Path

It is very obvious that the demands on the sales manager are increasing exponentially and that the types of skills and knowledge required to be successful are quite different from the past. The sales manager must act more like a general manager than ever before. The implications of this change go far beyond technology. For example, the sales manager must understand the business perspective, which means cross-functional experience. Sales managers must receive training in business techniques and marketing approaches so that they will be able to develop and implement sales strategies for their markets. Senior management must recognize these changes and reflect them in job descriptions, compensation, and decision latitude; otherwise, the pressures of the position will be converted into frustration and turnover.

In addition to assignments in other functions, sales managers need training in basic business analysis so that they can effectively utilize decision support software or other technology-based tools provided to them. Once the analytical and business models are understood, then training in the use of systems technology will be productive.

Sales Force Automation and the Field Manager

Many of the tools described in Chapter 8 related to field management, as well as the reps. Capabilities such as training, deployment, call targeting, reporting, forms, and electronic mail all represent powerful capabilities that assist the manager in communicating with his resources. There remains a need for decision support tools that help the manager to recognize exceptions and trends before the competition or before they otherwise hurt the business. Also, with greater emphasis on profitability, there is a need to help the manager to optimize programs and resources. Some of this type of decision making may need to remain in the domain of gut feel, but, at a minimum, corporate management must assist field managers with reasonable tools to interpret results and view the market as a business.

Endnotes

1. Mark Blessington and Bill O'Connell, *Sales Reengineering From the Outside In* (New York: McGraw-Hill, 1995), 230.

2. William A. O'Connell and William Keenan, Jr., "The Shape of Things to Come," *Sales & Marketing Management,* January 1990, 37–41.

3. Melissa Campanelli, "Can Managers Coach?" *Sales & Marketing Management,* July 1994, 59–66.

4. Melissa Campanelli, "What Price Sales Force Satisfaction?" *Sales & Marketing Management,* July 1994, 37.

5. William C. Johnson and Richard J. Chvala, *Total Quality in Marketing* (Delray Beach, FL: St. Lucie Press, 1996), 107.

6. Robert C. Blattberg and John Deighton, "Interactive Marketing: Exploiting the Age of Addressability," *Sloan Management Review,* Fall 1991, 12.

CHAPTER 10

SALES QUALITY

A New Concept?

The TQM movement that has swept across America over the past ten years has largely missed the sales function. Surveys estimate the percentage of companies that have extended their TQM program to include the sales function to be less than 10%. This is altogether understandable and unfortunate; if TQM represents a commitment to the delivery of quality goods and services to the customer, then how can sales not be included in this initiative? One can speculate that with a product-oriented mindset and with the geographical dispersion of the field sales force, most companies have essentially dismissed any role for the sales organization in TQM. On a less optimistic note, John Goodman, president of the Technical Assistance Research Program (TARP), has estimated that 60% of the quality improvement programs in the United States don't go beyond lip service. Goodman also points out that 80% of customer satisfaction depends on doing it right the first time, yet most companies spend 95% of their customer service time fixing problems.[1] This philosophy carries over to salespeople. It is not unusual for salespeople to spend a significant amount of contact time (phone or face-to-face) with customers dedicated to resolving supplier-related problems.

Chapter 3 presented a model that placed the sales function in the middle of the delivery of service and value to the customer. Given this model, how can one dismiss the importance of sales? Logically, the sales function needs to be an integral part of any TQM program. The Malcolm Baldrige Quality Award allocates 300 of the 1,000 total points to the sales and marketing area. Thus, quality professionals recognize that the linkage must occur to reach maximum results.

Sales force automation provides a number of capabilities that can enhance delivered quality and facilitate participation by the sales function. The purpose of this chapter is to raise the level of awareness of the opportunities and benefits of linkage between sales automation and quality.

Additional Perspective

Whether formally recognized or not, the sales function is a critical element of any organization's quality effort. Consider the following:

- A prospect's first impression of delivered quality is the salesperson on that first call.

- The salesperson interprets needs and converts them into products and services.

- The salesperson sets the customer's expectations.

- The salesperson has unique insights relative to value through the discussion of price and the emphasis of the prospective organization.

- The salesperson often becomes enmeshed in sorting out the problems when quality is not delivered.

- The salesperson positions the quality efforts of the company. If not personally involved, these efforts are merely features and benefits rather than a personal commitment.

What this implies is that despite Herculean effort elsewhere in the organization, the salesperson is the lynch pin in making it real for the customer. Further, if not actively involved in the quality program, it is difficult to comprehend how the salesperson will internalize it and make it real for the customer.

In an article based on a report generated by Learning International, the author provides a list of customer expectations of the sales relationship, including:[2]

- **Business expertise and image**: The salesperson needs to understand general business and economic trends, have good personal appearance and personality, understand the decision-making process within the customer's company, and know the competition.

- **Dedication to the customer**: A salesperson must be honest, help solve problems, be reachable when needed, take a long-term perspective in doing business, get the backing needed from his company, and suggest creative solutions to business problems.

- **Account sensitivity and guidance**: A salesperson must coordinate all aspects of a product or service to provide a total package, offer guidance throughout the sales process, instill confidence, be sensitive to a customer's pricing needs, respond to customer concerns, keep promises, and bring in others from the company to meet customer needs.

- **Partnership relationship**: Customers would like to view the sales rep as a virtual member of their own team rather than as a peddler. The biggest pitfall for companies that desire to market through consultative selling is an emphasis on making quarterly goals instead of taking a long-term view.

Reasons for Gaining/Losing Business

The following research statistics reinforce the importance of the sales/customer interface in gaining and keeping business:

- A study of buyers in the electrical utility industry found that credibility, reliability, and responsiveness were the most highly rated salesperson competencies and that "degree" of initiative taken was considered more important than friendship in making the sale.[3]

■ There are more than three times as many customers lost due to poor service than as a result of poor product performance.[4]

■ The following are factors in winning and losing business based on an international survey:[5]

Factors That Win Customers	Factors That Lose Customers
1. Capabilities	1. Trust
2. Trust	2. Quality
3. Price	3. Capabilities
4. Quality	4. Price

The high ranking of trust and capabilities suggests that the salesperson has considerable impact on the initial and on-going purchase decision. Both trust and capabilities are associated with the quality issue, as will be related in the discussion of companies that have implemented sales quality programs. Even for companies seeking to win the Baldrige Award, there appears to be a lack of connection between sales and customer satisfaction. In one survey, it was found that few firms actually pay their salespeople for customer satisfaction, even though 35–40% of them considered trying to win the Baldrige Award for Quality.[6]

A Model

The conceptual models presented in Chapters 4 and 5 demonstrate the linkage between the sales organization and internal resources and their combined effort in serving the customer. For simplicity, these relationships can be described as in Figure 10.1.

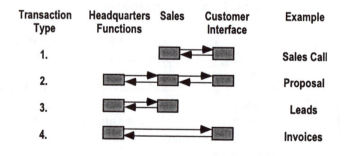

Transaction Type	Headquarters Functions	Sales	Customer Interface	Example
1.				Sales Call
2.				Proposal
3.				Leads
4.				Invoices

Figure 10.1   Examples of linkage processes between staff, sales, and the customer.

Each of these transactions involves quality. Using the examples provided in Figure 10.1, one can readily identify these quality characteristics and dependencies.

Transaction Type	Example	Quality
1.	Sales Call	Two-way flow of information involving the description of company offerings and getting feedback regarding customer needs and the way the customer likes to do business.
2.	Proposal	The quality (completeness) of the questions asked by the sales rep will define the response by the customer. The accuracy of the document used to convey the information to sales administration will influence the quality of the response to the sales rep. The sales rep then delivers the proposal or reworks it to meet the customer's expectations, thereby delaying its delivery.
3.	Leads	The quality of leads received by sales is reflected in how well they are qualified (index of quality) and in the quantity (sufficient to meet new business requirements). Marketing needs quality feedback from the field (timely and accurate in terms of reasons for rejection) so that the lead sourcing process can be improved.
4.	Invoices	The salesperson may not be directly involved with the invoicing process, but clearly, inaccurate invoices (quality) will cause delays in payment and administrative overload for the supplier and customer, a definite lose/lose.

Chapter 6 described sales force automation applications and how they can provide editing, simplify data capture, and leverage the capabilities of sales reps, so that they are less dependent on support organizations. The net of these capabilities is that they will improve quality as delivered within the supplier's organization and improve the quality of delivered service to the customer in terms of accuracy of information, timeliness, and relevance to the needs and expectations of the customer.

Examples of the Opportunity

Eastman Chemical

Eastman Chemical won the Baldrige Quality Award in 1993. Their program is highly customized to their approach to the market and is characterized by high-profile participation by sales reps. The quality program at Eastman starts with a review and assessment of customer relationships that, in turn, identifies opportunities for improvements and is used as a vehicle to initiate improvement projects and report them back to the customer.

The Eastman organization is segmented into ten separate divisions, and the sales organization essentially contracts with the divisions regarding meeting goals and implementing strategies. The salespeople are aligned by industry; therefore, a given salesperson will sell many products into a narrow set of industries. The company wants them to be industry experts.

The quality program referred to as MEPS (Make Eastman the Preferred Supplier) has as its objective: "Identify ways to improve the process that link us with our customer." MEPS projects are generally sales driven and always customer focused. Other functions "link in" with sales reps to work on customer-related problems. Thus, the sales rep is always involved with attempts to improve quality-related problems. In fact, the company encourages the sales reps to ask about problems and make it easy for customers to complain. Prior to the quality program, it would require the equivalent of three meetings to determine if a communication from a customer should be categorized as a complaint.

The company conducts an annual customer survey. The salesperson delivers the survey and picks it up. After the survey is analyzed, the sales rep reviews it with the customer to gain additional feedback, particularly where ratings are significantly better or worse than the nearest competitor.

When improvements are made, the Eastman sales rep communicates this fact to the customer to reinforce the commitment to continuous improvement and to ensure that the customer recognizes the value added. Although specific economic returns are unknown, Eastman has reported that claims and returns were reduced by 40% during the period 1992–93.

IBM Wisconsin

IBM won the Baldrige Award in 1990 and started to apply the successes gained primarily in the manufacturing area to other parts of the organization. The sales function was one of the last to be involved. IBM Wisconsin was one of the first business units to embrace the quality concept. Interestingly, the company did not pursue it because it was in trouble, but rather because it was uncertain how to continue its success. The vision for the organization was to not only sell computers to data centers, but also to help customers gain competitive advantage in the worldwide market.

To get the initiative off the ground, the organization recognized that it had to make changes to structure and policies. Otherwise, the infrastructure would swallow it up.

■ One quota was established for all six branches; the offices had to work as a team.

■ The number of managers was reduced to achieve a flatter organization.

■ An educational program was initiated to provide training in quality techniques.

■ A new compensation program was developed that rewarded revenue, customer satisfaction, process improvement, leadership, and skills development.

Not coincidentally, these same changes were also directly linked with customer survey results that indicated customers wanted reps with better skills and a company that was easier to do business with.

Another key development of the program was the decision to consolidate the resources within the technical consulting services group. Previously, specific resources had been assigned to each office, but this arrangement did not provide the best service for customers. Thus, the sales group decided to consolidate the resources; within six months, contract work revenue increased by more than 100%.

Dow Chemical Company

Similar to Eastman, Dow utilizes its salespeople to deliver and discuss customer surveys. The surveys cover product, service, and operational areas. They continue to work toward more open-ended questions so that they can better identify opportunities. According to Dow, 85% of their people never have direct contact with a customer. Thus, they have started using the surveys to teach their people to think about the customer.

Ethyl Corporation

Ethyl has initiated sales-led work teams that meet at regular intervals to discuss initiatives aimed at improving customer satisfaction. They have been in operation since 1992 and have been credited with improving the cycle time for such processes as product lead times and order/delivery/payment methods.

They have also developed a better means to integrate R&D in the development of specifications with customers. As importantly, the teams have increased morale and significantly increased the insight of both staff and field people regarding customer issues. The customers are also responding well to the initiative through higher survey results.

Moving Forward

The underpinnings of the quality movement are the control of variability and continuous improvement. For organizations that are embracing TQM, consistency is sought through vendor qualifying and partnering. For example, in the commodity chemical industry, products are considered to be interchangeable between suppliers from a quality standpoint; therefore, quality has moved to measuring service performance. Inconsistent performance in the service area ultimately is reflected in higher costs.

Unlike manufacturing, where materials and processes can be controlled, the sales environment is by definition subject to variability; thus, the goal of sales quality must be to maintain a consistent and predictable (quality) response. Sales automation affords the tools to achieve such a result, but this is not where the quality issue should end. The energy of TQM is embodied in continuous improvement, and the sales organization must be effectively linked with this process. Historically, the geographical dispersion of the sales force has been an impediment to involvement, but with innovations such as video conferencing, conference calls, electronic mail/notes, and the Internet, geographical distance becomes less of an issue.

The next hurdles to effectively engage the sales force are management resistance and motivation of the salespeople to participate. Essentially, these issues are directly related. Both management and the salespeople are concerned with making money (i.e., achieving revenue goals). Neither group is going to be interested in supporting a quality initiative if they are not convinced that it will generate higher productivity and earnings. The framework for satisfying these needs is tied to a strategy that addresses the following:

■ Define the opportunity and necessity for improving processes linked with the customer and sales.

■ Identify incentives and performance-related decisions that serve as a disincentive for sales involvement in quality initiatives or that motivate sales behavior which is contrary to delivering quality. For example, an incentive system that pays as orders are received rather than when the material is successfully installed will encourage salespeople to submit incomplete orders.

■ Install incentive and performance-related decision processes that involve the sales function in delivered quality (e.g., customer satisfaction ratings).

■ Develop training regarding quality concepts and improvement methodologies that engage the salespeople in an issue they have interest in. For example, topics could include negotiating skills or closing strategies.

■ Evaluate and develop methodologies that facilitate sales input and/or leadership in planing processes that impact the customer.

■ Establish teams involving salespeople to address customer-oriented problems.

Clearly, the opportunity to leverage sales in improvement processes is great, but it requires a combination of tools and setting the right environment. Certainly, any company that positions itself as "customer-centric" must give this aspect of quality serious consideration.

Endnotes

1. John Goodman, "The Nature of Customer Satisfaction," *Quality Progress,* February 1989, 37.

2. Madelyn R. Callahan, "What Customers Want," *Training & Development,* December 1992, 31–36.

3. S. Hayes and W. Harley, "How Buyers View Industrial Salespeople," *Industrial Marketing Management,* 18 (1989), 73–80.

4. H. James Harrington, *Total Improvement Management* (New York: McGraw-Hill, 1995), 145.

5. Ibid., 55.

6. Mark Blessington and Bill O'Connell, *Sales Reengineeering from the Outside In* (New York: McGraw-Hill, 1995), 170.

CHAPTER 11

A METHODOLOGY

The Track Record

Sales force automation has a checkered record in terms of success. Anecdotal data will lead one to believe that it is either the greatest invention since the wheel or it is a concept more difficult to achieve than "cold fusion." Numerous studies have shown comparable results–the majority of the installs are marginally successful.

Part of this disappointing record stems from (1) a tendency to start a project without clear success criteria and (2) the fact that every project involves different constituencies (sales reps, sales management, information management, marketing, senior management, etc.), each with a unique perspective and agenda. Therefore, there may be differing opinions regarding the same install.

Unfortunately, sales automation has fallen into the same trap that TQM, reengineering, and incentives (50s and 60s) have experienced. All of these programs are powerful concepts and contain effective tools, but if they are approached from the standpoint of representing "silver bullets," success is very unlikely. The sales automation industry is an amalgam of software, hardware, and services, but the primary driver is software; therefore, the focus is on technology and the merits of the technology. The reality is that results are gained through the integration of technology with business processes so that they achieve competitive advantage for the user organization. Automation projects that have been initiated and principally sponsored by the IS function have minimal probability for success. This has nothing to do with competency; rather it speaks to the issue of who owns the system and the commitment to make it work.

Despite the horror stories, companies continue to embrace the technology and place the cart before the horse (technology driving the business). It is easy to become enamored by the capability of the technology and the potential "brass ring" it offers from a performance standpoint. The thrust of this chapter outlines an approach that provides a business rationale for automation and comprehends risk so that issues can be managed up front. The intent of this chapter is not to provide a detailed road map on this subject, because that would require more than one chapter; rather, it provides an understanding of the general conduct of the project. Chapter 13 will discuss organizational issues in greater depth. This chapter will describe a basic process without much detail regarding the project players.

Leadership vs. Management

Before embarking on a discussion of methodology, it is important to make a distinction in terms and perspective. A *methodology* infers a process that helps one reach an end point in an efficient manner. In this respect, the methodology in this chapter will maintain that context; however, this methodology is structured to gain senior management and end-user sponsorship and support.

Methodologies are important because they help to maintain discipline, keep the project on track, and address issues in their proper order. There is a distinct danger, however, in becoming overly fixated on the management (time and cost) aspects of the project and losing track of the true end point—a system that is used effectively. For example, an implementation team for a multi-billion-dollar company decided to shortcut the training program because their budget funding was running low at the end of the project. The result was less-than-effective training and a high incidence of calls to the system help line. Senior management was unhappy about the results and discussed the training program with the supplier. The upshot of the discussion was that the project team had been more concerned with meeting their budget and did not want to request additional funding. Senior management had access to several million dollars in a training budget, at least some of which could have been used for the project. In addition to a failure to communicate, the team obviously lost track of the more important objective—end-user acceptance and use of the system. It is also a prime example of doing what's right vs. that which is expedient.

Sales automation remains a very complex combination of business, technology, and human factors. Methodologies, just like technology, cannot be allowed to take on a life of their own. These comments are not meant to knock management of projects, because there is ample opportunity to waste a great deal of time and money; however, successful projects require leadership and an understanding of what constitutes reasonable trade-offs.

Overview

Although it is possible for companies to explore sales automation out of a specific need that they cannot reconcile (e.g., merging two sales forces, rapid rollout of new products, rapid deployment of new sales resources, etc.), the majority of companies approach the technology out of concerns regarding competitive advantage or concerns regarding productivity. At the point of inquiry, most organizations have limited insight regarding benefits and certainly have limited insight regarding potential costs or impact on the organization. As will be discussed in Chapter 12, even after talking with vendors, it is unlikely that an accurate appreciation of costs exists at this point.

Given that the commitment for a system is likely to be a six- to eight-figure investment (assumes a large sales force), a prudent strategy is to invest relatively small amounts of money to refine the estimate of costs and benefits while reducing the risk associated with these assessments. Graphically, this relationship can be described as indicated in Figure 11.1.

In this diagram, Phase 1 pertains to activities that define business needs and articulates a plan which incorporates recommendations for change that include technology and process change. Given that Phase 1 includes a full implementation plan, it is not difficult to visualize that elements of risk would drop disproportionately to the cost of conducting the study. The assumption is that Phase 1 is essentially a "go/no-go"

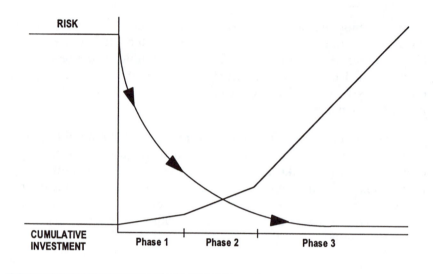

Figure 11.1   Project risk curve.

decision point. Senior management, fully informed regarding the costs, benefits, and risks associated with the project, elects to fund and staff the endeavor.

Phase 2 represents design, development, and piloting of the system. Due to the higher costs of development, the investment curve increases at a faster rate than in Phase 1. The risk curve is reduced disproportionately because unknowns regarding systems details and end-user acceptance are resolved. Given that the pilot had specific operational expectations, Phase 2 ends with a decision point to proceed, change scope, or stop.

Phase 3 represents a rollout of the pilot capabilities. The investment curve again increases in rate and magnitude because "per copy" versions of the system and hardware are being issued to the field. Note that the risk curve becomes very flat in this phase because the risk factors are largely managed out of the project and the remaining factors are associated with logistics. Thus, risk becomes lowest and most susceptible to good management when investment is the highest.

Granted, this is an idealized description of the process, but it does provide the rationale for a phased approach for these projects.

The Process

Figure 11.2 provides a diagram of the major elements of the process.

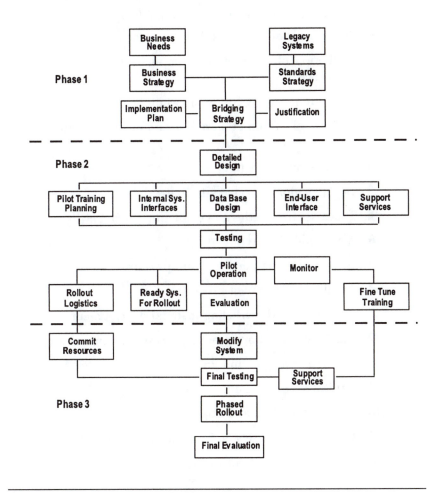

Figure 11.2   Overview of methodology.

Phase 1: Needs Assessment

The objective of the needs assessment is to establish a solid business rationale for automation and establish an implementation plan that embraces costs, resources, and risks. It is incumbent on senior management to evaluate the merits of investing in sales force automation vs. other opportunities. Typically, this decision is made at the "board level."

The needs assessment should address the following:

- Assessment of processes that touch the customer
- Definition of the sales process and evaluation of its relevance
- Definition of what customers want
- Review of customer base vs. competitor's customer base
- Competitive strategies
- Segmentation by value attributes
- Processes involved with channel management
- Value added represented by channel
- Sales/marketing interfaces and processes
- Product development processes
- Promotion and marketing material development
- Planning and administrative processes within sales
- Business strategies and goals
- Critical success factors
- Long-range plans and objectives
- Operational budgets and current spending levels
- Incentive and bonus structures

The review of these areas will provide insight regarding opportunities to:

- Reduce process cycle times
- Reduce costs
- Increase productivity
- Increase revenue

- Increase margins
- Reduce risk (e.g., retain customer base)

At this point in the process, it is useful to identify relevant sales force automation applications and develop estimates of their unique impact on the processes outlined above. These opportunities need to be integrated with a 3- to 5-year business plan to determine their potential contribution to meeting stated objectives. In general, it is useful to use a technique referred to as "gap analysis." As indicted in Figure 11.3, gap analysis is a tool used in strategic planning that defines the "gap" between where the organization wants to be vs. where it is likely to be without change. Classical gap analysis will include a series of recommendations that are intended to close the gap. In the case of sales automation, these recommendations will address the applications and processes referenced earlier.

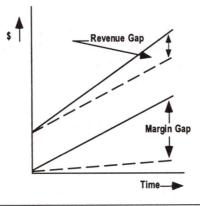

Figure 11.3   Gap analysis concentrating on revenue and margin generation.

The applications identified on the business side are the starting point for a review of legacy systems. Each application must be traced to systems that it may impact. Each system must be reviewed from the perspective of platform, databases, and interfaces. In addition, the systems strategy must be reviewed to identify planned changes to the systems potentially impacted by the sales automation applications and choice of platform moving forward.

Once the systems information is in place, it is possible to define the framework for a system. The elements of information that should be available at this time include:

■ The strategic implications of the system

■ Identity of processes that need to be revised or reengineered

■ Legacy system implications

■ Project team requirements

■ Resource requirements

■ Supplier recommendations

■ Projected benefits, project justification, and risks

■ Proposed timetable

This information needs to be reviewed by senior management and then "packaged" for submission to the board of directors for approval. During the Phase 1 process, it is essential to carefully note key dates that are critical to keeping the project on track:

1. Capital budget cycle dates. It is essential to include the project in the budget for the anticipated budget year of the rollout.

2. Dates for board of directors' meetings and due dates for project approval and review.

3. Any key dates relative to pilot or rollout (e.g., national meetings or periods when demand is less pressing).

Obviously, the intent is to work backwards from these key events to map out the target timetable.

Phase 2: The Pilot

Having secured approval for the project, the work proceeds toward detailed design, development of the applications, and the start-up of a pilot. This phase of the project requires many different types of disciplines because not only is systems design work commencing, but user interfaces, training, and support for the pilot are being planned and developed. Vendors need to be selected and efforts coordinated.

During this development work, pilot participants must be chosen and briefed as to timing and expectations. Since the pilot is essentially going to represent the launch pad for an eventual rollout, it is desirable to choose groups that possess the range of traits that will be experienced in the rollout. It is important that the pilot groups understand the time commitments and the potential for downside events. The pilot group must feel that they can be brutally honest but hopefully not get carried away in detail. Criteria for evaluating the pilot needs to be established before the pilot group is briefed, because data may need to be accumulated by the pilot group prior to the start of the pilot as a "before" benchmark.

People who are responsible for delivering the training should, if possible, attend the user interface design meetings. In this manner, they will learn the details of the interface and the rationale for certain design choices. End users should be utilized for the design of the interface and the navigational aspects of the system. These people should not be from the pilot group because the evaluation will be biased by potential "ownership" of the design and training decisions.

Support services for the pilot include:

- Preparing equipment for the pilot, including loading software, files, etc.

- Providing a spare pool and hardware replacement/repair procedures.

- Preparing help desk functions to answer questions and determine if there are problems with the system.

All of these mechanisms need to be in place prior to the pilot to determine readiness for the pilot. If the pilot is to accurately simulate rollout conditions, then everything needs to be tested, including dry runs, to reduce elements of risk.

Once the pilot training is complete, a debrief needs to occur so that during the pilot, modifications can be made and tested. At the end of the pilot, a complete debrief must occur, where every aspect of the program is evaluated for readiness. Success criteria for the pilot are evaluated, and the project team must make a recommendation relative to readiness for rollout.

Phase 3: The Rollout

As the process diagram indicates, unless there is a desire for a significant interval between the end of the pilot and the start of the rollout, planning, training, and ramp-up of resources must be done while the pilot is in operation. This is another reason why the pilot must be rigorous; without this discipline, it will be difficult to make decisions regarding the adequacy of the pilot approaches.

The pilot duration should be used as a window to fine tune all aspects of the logistics of the rollout. If new resources are involved, they need to go through complete dry runs to ensure readiness for the rollout. A flaw in a pilot is surmountable, but a flaw in a rollout can be devastating to the credibility of the program.

At the end of the rollout, there needs to be a final evaluation. This point represents a critical juncture for the project and the people who worked on it. Internal resources are reassigned, and some organizations make a critical error in assuming that, once in place, the system will transition to autopilot. Sales automation systems must retain relevance with the marketplace. An effective champion for the system must remain in place after the rollout to ensure issues are addressed, changes are made as required, and new features are added (as requested by the field). It is possible to do everything right and lose the benefits for the organization by removing the champion.

CHAPTER 12

COSTS AND JUSTIFICATION

Costs vs. Benefits

The complexity of sales force automation seems to drive people to seek a means to net it out to some composite measure. Over the years, the surrogate measure has been cost. This is unfortunate because it again positions the technology as though one were making a decision for the sales fleet. This could not be further from the truth or at least should be far from the truth. As will be discussed and documented, if justification is an issue, there is something dramatically wrong with the perspective. What is equally ironic is the lack of consistency regarding the per-user cost numbers shared within the industry. The following notes but a few examples of this discrepancy:

- The Conference Board uses a number of $5,000/rep as a median cost including hardware, software, training, and upgrades.[1]

- A survey sponsored by Dell Computers placed the number at $6,400/rep.

- *Client/Server Magazine* places the number at $15,000/rep with maintenance costs of $3,500/rep per year.[2]

- A Culpepper White Paper places the cost at $10,000–12,000/rep.[3]

- The Sales Automation Association's Paul Seldon uses a figure of $12,000–17,000/rep with maintenance costs of $2,000–2,500/rep per year.[4]

All of these numbers are analogous to providing an answer before knowing the question. The cost per rep is a function of a great many factors. Consider the following:

1. How many users will be on the system? The number of users strongly influences average cost because there are sizable fixed costs involved. For example, system development cost and training curriculum development are essentially fixed costs.

2. Is the system networked?

3. How extensively is the system integrated with legacy systems?

4. What are the types and breadth of applications?

5. Where is the laptop of choice relative to product life cycle? The spread here is about $3,000–7,000.

6. Are custom applications involved?

7. Is the question being asked in the context of initial applications or total applications.

8. Does the number reflect total outsourcing of development?

9. What support services are considered?

Unfortunately, customers ask the questions and vendors feel compelled to answer. Concerned about frightening the prospect or appearing to lack value, vendors tend to provide low end numbers that set expectations and result in a chain of events that tend to serve no one.

An Almost Complete List of Costs

It is very difficult to identify *every* cost for *every* type of company/ industry. The following list identifies the major elements of the typical phased installation. Obviously, each phase will have a corresponding cost. Each company has different attitudes regarding the inclusion of internal resources in project costs. Note that typically there will be an internal project manager and an external project manager representing one or more vendors; project management will be mentioned in each section, as well as project team members.

Needs Assessment

- Resources
    - ❖ Project manager(s)
    - ❖ Project team (internal and external members)
    - ❖ Field sales time

- Field "work withs"

- Customer interviews

- Meeting days

- Travel costs

- Presentation material

- Software/hardware for demonstration purposes

- Notes: Travel costs can be exceptionally high during this phase. Field input is essential, which means people are going out to the field or field people are coming in for group discussion.

System Design and Development

- ■ Resources
  - ❖ Project manager(s)
  - ❖ Project team (internal and external members)
  - ❖ Travel
  - ❖ Field sales time

- ■ User system
  - ❖ Functional specifications
  - ❖ Design specifications
  - ❖ Development (iterative process)
  - ❖ Laptop computers and software
  - ❖ Testing
  - ❖ Documentation

- ■ Server system
  - ❖ Functional specifications
  - ❖ Design specifications
  - ❖ Development
  - ❖ Server, software, and modems
  - ❖ Installation of communication lines
  - ❖ Communications costs
  - ❖ Testing
  - ❖ Documentation

- ■ Database
  - ❖ Functional specifications
  - ❖ Design specifications
  - ❖ Development

- ❖ Software
- ❖ Testing
- ❖ Documentation
- ■ Interface with legacy systems
  - ❖ Functional specifications
  - ❖ Design specifications
  - ❖ Development
  - ❖ Software
  - ❖ Hardware/software to link systems
  - ❖ Testing
  - ❖ Documentation
  - ❖ Notes: Critical aspects of this phase are that the end-user interface design process is iterative; there can be many meetings and much travel associated with this activity. Although the connection to the legacy systems is referred to as an interface, the reality is that these systems may require more than a simple utility program to extract or add data. Major funding can be involved in this area.

Pilot Preparation

- ■ Resources
  - ❖ Project manager(s)
  - ❖ Project team (internal and external members)
  - ❖ Travel
  - ❖ Field sales time
- ■ Training concept and materials
  - ❖ Define training content and approach
  - ❖ Develop training scenarios (day-in-the-life concept)

- ❖ Document approach and produce materials

- ❖ Conduct dry runs

- ❖ Define training site requirements, review the adequacy of the pilot training location, and test communication capabilities

- ❖ Finalize materials

- ❖ Notes: Companies typically underestimate their training budgets by a factor of four. Include cost factors such as salesperson costs, instructor costs, facilities costs, and materials costs.

■ Data preparation

- ❖ Convert data to load into modules

- ❖ Testing

- ❖ Notes: This step includes E-mail lists, customer data, reference information, etc. Any type of information that can be pre-loaded in the software should be loaded to minimize the administrative requirements of the system. At the pilot stage, this conversion may be a more manual process, and the insight gained should guide the rollout methodology. Some input by the reps will inevitably be required, but even in this respect, there should be a time frame to complete it.

■ Purchase hardware, accessories, and software

- ❖ Notes: From a budget standpoint, this can be tricky; the purchase will likely include more users than the field pilot group. Other people will need to be on the system, such as project people, help-line workers, and perhaps other staff groups, depending on the nature of the applications. Spare equipment will also be needed to cover equipment that fails. If changes in process are involved, steps must be taken to accommodate modifications for pilot evaluation and plans for the rollout.

■ Prepare hardware

> ❖ Burn-in of equipment to reduce potential of field failures or DOAs at training

> ❖ Load software and data

> ❖ Add accessories

> ❖ Test software and communications

> ❖ Repackage (return to original packaging and over-wrap to provide a sales rep unit)

> ❖ Ship to training sites

> ❖ Notes: This set of activities can be full of surprises. Equipment and software fail. There might be high costs for preparation and shipping. There must be secure places to store the equipment during preparation and at the training site.

■ Establish services

> ❖ Define requirements (hours of coverage, escalation, repair turnaround time, etc.)

> ❖ Select vendor(s) and/or recruit internal resources

> ❖ Train help-line staff regarding configuration and unique applications

> ❖ Add full-time IS staff to run the system (may not be necessary)

> ❖ Inventory all equipment and set up tracking database

> ❖ Notes: The pilot is a live operation. It needs to be complete so that the adequacy of the capabilities can be evaluated prior to rollout. The intent should be to avoid surprises at rollout. The implication of this is that operational costs will start to kick in even before the pilot starts; these costs will be disproportionately higher than the rollout because of economies of scale.

■ Define success criteria for the pilot

Pilot Operation

- Resources
  - ❖ Project manager(s)
  - ❖ Project team (internal and external members)
  - ❖ Travel
  - ❖ Field sales time
  - ❖ Trainers and services support
  - ❖ Training facility costs
  - ❖ Operational costs including communication costs, support services, etc.
  - ❖ IS operations staff

- Conduct training

- Evaluate training

- Conduct field "work withs"

- Formal evaluation of the pilot from an operational and performance standpoint

- Evaluate readiness for rollout

- Rerun, extend, expand pilot based on results

- Report readiness for rollout to senior management

- Notes: The pilot operation is critical to success. It is important not to allow schedules to get in the way of making sure that the methodology is right. The costs to fix problems once they reach the field are staggering, not to mention the loss in credibility. Also note that when a pilot is set up, it typically stays in operation while preparations are made for the rollout. This means that the operating costs continue during this period.

Modification of Systems/Services

- ■ Resources
  - ❖ Project manager(s)
  - ❖ Project team (internal and external members)
  - ❖ Travel
  - ❖ Field sales time
  - ❖ Trainers and services support
  - ❖ Training facility costs
  - ❖ Operational costs including communication costs, support services, etc.
  - ❖ IS operations staff
  - ❖ Notes: Feedback from the pilot may reveal flaws in the system that need to be corrected before the pilot is launched. Sometimes these are modest in scope and can be handled during the pilot operation. Depending on the nature of the change, it may be wise to rerun or expand the pilot group to evaluate the merits of the change before rollout. These are judgment calls, but from a budgeting standpoint, failure to comprehend such an event will easily violate budget and time-frame estimates.

Ramp Up for the Rollout

- ■ Resources
  - ❖ Project manager(s)
  - ❖ Project team (internal and external members)
  - ❖ Travel
  - ❖ Field sales time
  - ❖ Trainers and services support
  - ❖ Training facility costs

- ❖ Operational costs including communication costs, support services, etc.
- ❖ IS operations staff

■ Develop logistics plan

- ❖ Training sites and schedules (may involve site visits)
- ❖ Trainers and train-the-trainer schedule
- ❖ Equipment and software purchase schedule; a secure area for holding prior to rollout
- ❖ Location, throughput, and resources to meet rollout schedule
- ❖ Shipment logistics to coordinate equipment with training sites
- ❖ Coordination of events with the field
- ❖ Quality control to ensure smooth operation

■ Train the trainers

- ❖ Interview and select trainers
- ❖ Train the trainers
- ❖ Schedule dry runs to determine readiness

■ Equipment and software preparation

- ❖ Receive equipment and software, enter in database, and secure for use
- ❖ Prepare equipment for rollout training
- ❖ Load software and data and repack
- ❖ Ship to training sites according to schedule

■ Communicate the schedule, expectations, etc. with the organization as a whole

- Coordinate training schedule
  - ❖ Field users
  - ❖ Trainers
  - ❖ Internal staff users
  - ❖ Service providers

Execute Rollout

- Resources
  - ❖ Project manager(s)
  - ❖ Project team (internal and external members)
  - ❖ Travel
  - ❖ Field sales time
  - ❖ Trainers and services support
  - ❖ Training facility costs
  - ❖ Operational costs including communications costs, support services, etc.
  - ❖ IS operations staff

- Notify senior management of readiness

- Notes: It is wise to maintain a modest back-up group at headquarters that can scrabble to solve or correct any problems experienced in the field, including sudden illness of trainers.

Post-Rollout Review

- Resources
  - ❖ Project manager(s)
  - ❖ Project team (internal and external members)
  - ❖ Travel

❖ Field sales time

❖ Trainers and services support

❖ Training facility costs

❖ Operational costs including communication costs, support services, etc.

❖ IS operations staff

■ Establish a punch list of outstanding issues and set up plans for corrective action

■ Evaluate performance of the rollout

■ Monitor usage of the system

■ Conduct spot "work withs" to evaluate system or organizational issues that need attention

■ Report results to senior management

■ Celebrate!

■ Set up plans to reabsorb internal project resources

■ Notes: Again, from a budget standpoint, there must be a clear agreement as to when the project mode is over and the operational mode is in place. Project resources may require time to reabsorb, so the project budget needs to reflect a continuation of resources to take care of loose ends and the reabsorption process.

On-Going Maintenance

■ Resources

❖ Project champion (may be part-time)

❖ Operational resources

❖ Support services

❖ Training for new users

❖ Administrator(s) to maintain the system

❖ Operational budget

❖ Project budget to expand and enhance the system based on the original plan

❖ Capital budget to include new users

❖ Communication budget to relate issues regarding success stories, etc.

Justification

If the project is initiated with a well-executed business needs assessment, then the rationale for implementation will be based on sound logic and business principles. As will be discussed in this section, identifying areas of improvement is not difficult; what tends to be difficult is establishing cause and effect in subsequent performance. Field sales is not a test tube environment. There are some issues like head count and expenses that are well defined, but others, particularly as they apply to revenue and margin, are often more difficult to isolate. There is a distinct danger of not seeing "the forest for the trees." If one examines each issue discreetly, a fault will undoubtedly be found. But if one considers the totality of the project, then it is more reasonable to believe that the collective effect will be positive. Thus, the justification must consider the entire impact to be fair to the project.

At the same time, it must be realized that the sales automation project must compete against other worthwhile projects that have significant impact for the organization. Projects in manufacturing and operations are typically well documented and the return well measured; therefore, the justification for a project must be comprehensive in scope and analysis in terms of planning and business implications. As with project costs, it is beyond the scope of this book to identify every potential source of justification; it is intended to stimulate thinking and provide the reader with a starting place.

Justification of systems typically addresses the following five basic business considerations:

1. **Strategic Issues**: These issues relate to capabilities that are considered essential to future success (e.g., decentralized decision making, consolidation of sales forces, sophisticated new product lines, rapid release of new products, expansion into new industries, etc.). The justification strategy is to link the capabilities to these requirements, thereby improving their impact or reducing the risk/cost of achieving them. A strategic issue will have revenue and cost components; however, the emphasis here is positioning the system as an enabler to transition the organization to some future state faster and with less risk than alternatives.

   According to a McKinsey and Company study, products that go to market six months late but within budget earn 33% less than expected. Products that go to market on time but 50% over budget earn only 4% less than expected.[5] Sales automation is not going to singularly reduce product development cycle; however, automation offers opportunity to provide better input regarding customer priorities and can speed market penetration through improved training and call targeting.

   In 1991 a government study found that practitioners of the Baldrige criteria enjoyed average improvements of 8.6% in sales per employee, gained 13.7% in market share, and increased customer satisfaction by 2.5%.[6] Although the study does not provide a cause-and-effect linkage, it is reasonable to assume that the Baldrige Award provides leverage when trying to enter new markets. With existing customers, however, it is the improvement in overall service performance that is the driver. This reinforces the notion of improving the processes that directly impact the customer.

2. **Revenue Growth**: How will the system impact revenue growth based on the assumptions regarding where and how that growth is going to be achieved? Note that this concept also considers the issue of market share (revenue growth relative to market growth).

3. **Margins**: Used as a separate context, margin is meant to capture issues regarding pricing and use of discounts, allowances, etc. It is also meant to cover issues regarding product mix and profitability.

4. **Costs**: Cost reduction mean using less of a resource or avoiding the need to add head count (cost avoidance).

5. **Risk**: Risk is a qualitative factor that is sometimes handled as a percentage. Risk should be viewed as having an up side and a down side. Every company handles this issue somewhat differently; however, a form of scenario analysis (i.e., what-if situations) is often used to provide a tangible sense of the risk involved.

Sales force automation systems involve a significant investment in expense and capital. The order of magnitude of the investment is determined at the board of directors level. Therefore, everything rests on the quality of the justification and the support of senior executives who will place their credibility on the line. It will be very rough going if the project was not included in the current year's capital budget. Thus, early in the process, it is useful to have a financial person on the team who knows the mechanics of the capital budget and project approval processes.

Sources of Improvement

Strategic Issues

These types of issues are often associated with critical success factors—long-range plans or even annual reports. The following examples provide insight regarding the nature of some common needs and their relationship to sales force automation. Since strategic issues are sometimes more compelling than pure economic impact, they can be key to achieving approval. If a company does not have long-range plans, that is scary in itself. The end of this section will offer some suggestions for dealing with this possibility.

■ **Decentralization**: This is a management strategy that seeks to move decision making to its lowest practical level. It is a form of empowerment; success in this area includes, among other things, the correct decision tools and overall account-ability. Sales automation applications can provide remote users with effective tools and feedback systems to facilitate this process. Pricing decisions and local promotion funding are good examples of this type of need.

Owens Corning Building Supply Division, a building sup-ply manufacturer located in Toledo, OH, implemented a sales automation system that does away with bureaucracy and empowers salespeople to make more decisions on their own. The system includes word processing, presentations, product information, most commonly used tech bulletins, customer specifications, pricing information, customer buying history, types of products ordered, and preferred payment plans. This data had previously been stored in loose-leaf binders, calendars, and account cards. Field management has been reduced by half, and Corning cut out a layer of senior management at the beginning of 1994. Support staff has also been cut in satellite offices. In pre-automation days, it was the managers who looked for the problem orders, dealt with customer complaints, and resolved issues. The salespeople now do this faster because they have all the data available. They can prepare themselves for calls, transmit orders elec-tronically, access pre-written letters, and send pamphlets, brochures, and other materials to clients via a centralized administrative function. Managers now manage people and accounts. Automation allows sales managers to see what is going on as it happens and to react quickly to change strategies as necessary. As the span of control increases, the managers will handle fewer accounts and become respon-sible for more training. According to Corning, their real intent was not cost reduction as much as increased attention to customers. By removing layers of bureaucracy, they improved cost and response time.[7]

- ■ **Performance Criteria**: One of the trends that is occurring in the marketplace today is the inclusion of profit and customer satisfaction criteria in sales performance plans. The effectiveness of these changes is directly related to how much control sales reps feel they have over these issues. In some cases, it may mean effective feedback regarding product mix and profit, while in other cases, it may mean the ability to add value to the customer.

Swissôtel needed to increase revenue by 35% but did not see how they could achieve that growth without adding significant staff. In reviewing the time allocation of field sales reps, it was noted that the reps spent the majority of their time preparing proposals, writing contracts, and preparing expenses. In approaching the design of a system, one of the key insights was that if properly equipped, the salespeople did not have to be property based. The support system could provide them with immediate availability information, and by providing better staff support, the administrative time could be dramatically reduced. Since the installation of the system, they have hit a 35% growth rate without adding field resources.[8]

■ **New Product Introductions**: Most companies are seeking to reduce product development cycle time and speed up the frequency of release of new products. This strategy infers that the sales organization is going to be able to learn and effectively sell the new products, correctly target prospects, and build the market while maintaining the current customers. Sales automation applications can include training, targeting, and sales process management capabilities to support this type of strategy.

For example, Storage Technologies, a $1 billion computer data storage company, was preparing to launch fourteen new products when a survey discovered that salespeople spent the majority of their time performing administrative tasks and less than one-third of their time selling. In addition, it was discovered that sales process cycle time and proposal generation time were unacceptably high. Through sales automation, the company was able to increase selling time by 50% and reduce the sales process cycle by 25%, thereby facilitating the new product releases and positioning the company for rapid implementation of future releases.

Gerber Baby Care Products Division, located in Fremont, MI, implemented a sales automation system that has trimmed four weeks off the time it takes to get new products into the pipeline. Additional benefits include:

❖ Advertising campaigns are now being mapped with considerably less built-in waste.

❖ Reps now spend 5% of their time on administrative tasks and phone usage vs. the industry standard of 12%.

❖ Sales management administrative time is reduced from 22% to 10%.

❖ Paperwork reduction saved field reps 8 hours a week and division managers up to 16 hours per week.

❖ The company now sells outside brand products in order to boost the company's cash flow (could have reduced the field staff by 10%).

❖ The company also uses syndicated data to aid retailers in their marketing and sales efforts.

❖ Gerber also uses scanner forms to record planogram layouts and compare to optimal rated stores based on merchandising effectiveness.

❖ Gerber has a program to determine how often reps should go into accounts. They also look for opportunities to exploit a competitor's mis-step.

❖ Customers and Gerber's marketing department are provided with actionable data.

❖ All sales reps can communicate faster with each other, sales management, and marketing. This can be a key capability when, for example, distribution is not near proper levels pending a major advertising drive.

❖ Point-of-purchase sales information can be collected in a timely manner.

❖ Performance and results can be measured accurately.

❖ If there is a promotion requiring a 70% distribution and they see they are nowhere close, they can look at options.[9]

■ **Redeploy Sales Resources by Industry**: This is a common strategy of the 90s that is solution or value oriented. Solution selling is likely to require knowledge of the industry; if the current structure is product oriented, this type of change can be traumatic. Sales automation can be used as a vehicle to provide training with regard to industries, solutions, and products to help reduce the learning curve. Other tools such as selling tools or bulletin boards can leverage the current knowledge base of the organization.

■ **Combining Sales Forces**: Most customers do not want to be called on by an army of salespeople representing the same company. Procter and Gamble had over 20 salespeople calling on their largest accounts. The obvious question is how to retain focus and yet provide a capability to deal with a broad product line. Training, communications, product reference material, and account planning are key capabilities under these circumstances.

■ **Channel Management**: The more complex the channel structure, the more difficult it is to avoid conflicts and evaluate performance. Communication tools and electronic linkage with the sales force and the headquarters location can reduce administrative overhead while producing smooth interfaces and cooperation.

■ **Responsiveness**: Many companies realize that they must reduce cycle time on the majority of their customer interfaces. Unfortunately, the goals tend to be obscure. The applications described in Chapter 6 have the capability of dramatically reducing cycle time for processes such as design, order entry, literature fulfillment, and quotes. Another aspect of responsiveness is the ability to respond to changes in the marketplace. This type of responsiveness has two components: one is effectively reading the market, and the other is creating and implementing a response. Sales automation opens new avenues of communication and provides for a rapid transfer of market-related data. On the flip side, sales automation can provide training, sales tools, and call targeting capabilities that can shrink implementation time.

In 1987, Frito-Lay, Inc., located in Plano, TX, took the bold step of providing 10,000 hand-helds for its route sales staff. Data from the network is used to determine what shelf space needs to be filled, where products are getting stale, and how to adjust delivery days to meet each customer's requirements. The company can monitor snack food sales and trends in 48 hours. The system saves more than $20 million in operations costs per year.[10]

A study by the Forum Corporation concluded that an undifferentiated product can command up to a 10% price premium when supported by outstanding service.[11]

Nalco Chemical's primary goal in automating their sales force has been to make the sales reps more efficient by being able to work untethered from support staff. Customer surveys have indicated that 53% of customers indicated that the use of notebook computers was a factor in staying with Nalco. The company estimated this survey result equates to $24 million in business saved.[12]

In their book *Time-Based Competition,* George Stalk, Jr. and Thomas Hout provide the following benchmark improvements based on time-based competition:[13]

❖ Prices are 10–100% higher.

❖ Manufacturing and service costs are 10–20% lower.

❖ Product and service development costs are 30–50% lower.

❖ Inventory turns are two to four times higher.

❖ Revenue-to-plant and equipment investment ratios are 50% higher.

❖ Net asset turns are two times higher.

The reason for including this reference is to reinforce the domino effect of improvements throughout the organization. There is enormous leverage in time compression.

Most companies will not have these issues articulated as neatly as defined above. To identify these issues and bring them to the surface requires asking the right open-ended questions regarding current and future challenges. As the needs are identified, it should be possible to recast them in directional terms as outlined above. It is desirable to look for discontinuities in the numbers and the plans among functions such as manufacturing, marketing, and sales. Turnover and attracting high-caliber recruits are other areas to consider. If the organization has a vision statement, that can prove to be very effective in tapping into the emotional fabric of the company.

Bank of America Mortgage, a division of Bank America, Uniondale, NY, has deployed a sales automation system for its 200 loan officers to be used to order credit reports, print out applications, and find out the status of mortgage processing on the spot. The bank has been able to take three days out of the mortgage application process. This has created the impression of innovation in the marketplace. The system allows the loan officers to sift through 50 or more variations of mortgage programs to find which one is right for the customer; thus, the system has created a new service.[14]

Productivity Issues

Productivity is a measurement of performance that is based on a ratio of a measure of output divided by a measure of input (e.g., tonnage sold per sales rep, revenue dollars per sales rep, and sales calls per close). What is particularly useful about productivity measures is that one can relate items with completely different unit values. As a ratio, any number by itself is meaningless, but if a trend is established, then one can see directional improvement. The vulnerability of this analysis is that shifts in the numbers can occur for reasons not related to productivity (e.g., price increases, product mix, etc.). On the positive side, productivity measures can provide a useful method for netting out change. For example, it may be possible to increase sales using a more expensive mix of resources that are in different cost centers; the productivity figure would then reflect this diminished performance.

■ **Lead Management**: The management of leads utilizes ratios to determine effectiveness. Measures such as percentage of qualified leads and qualified leads per close are indicators of how efficient the lead generation process is at attracting the right prospects. In an article by Robyn Griggs entitled "Taking the Leads," the author provides some mind-boggling statistics:[15]

❖ Studies have shown that sales force follow-up rates on leads quadruple from 10–39% when a structured lead management system is in place.

❖ A Cahners Publishing Co. survey suggests that only 15% of business and industrial inquiries ever result in a salesperson's call.

❖ An estimated 76% of those who inquire about a product or service intend to buy and 40% don't bother to approach the competition. Roughly 63% of all leads turn into a sale for someone.

❖ Robot Research, a San Diego-based company, established a formal telemarketing program to qualify leads, and sales jumped by 9%. The value of each lead jumped from $1.27 to $8.57 per dollar invested in leads.

■ **Win/Lose Ratios:** A critical statistic for most organizations is the win vs. lose statistic. If properly documented, it can be used to monitor the competitive environment and sharpen sales tactics. The key is to document the event, the circumstances, and the competition.

■ **Sales Rep Time Utilization**: Productivity increases through improved time availability have been a bedrock basis for justification of sales automation for many years. To demonstrate this rationale, assume that typical sales reps distribute their time as follows:

Activity	Percent of Total Time
Sales time	25
Travel	25
Administration	20
Meetings/training	10
Problem resolution	20
Total	100

The first question that needs to be asked is whether these numbers reflect total time dedicated to the job or time as it relates to potential call time. The implication is that if the numbers relate to dedicated time, then any reallocation of time based on a reduction of administrative time is going to represent a trade-off between personal time and available call time. Under these circumstances, any significant reallocation to call time would be tenuous.

Assuming that the time allocation represents potential call time, then it is reasonable to assume some net gain. For the sake of illustration, if administration could be reduced to 10%, can one assume a net productivity increase of 10%? The answer to this question is "probably not." The reasoning is as follows; if the sales rep is maximizing time available by providing proper coverage to "A" accounts, then more time may not be useful. This leaves "B and C" level accounts. Covering these accounts may deliver incremental benefits, but it is unlikely that they will be at the same rate as the average, and a certain amount of coverage will be reflected in travel. Thus, it will not be a one-for-one translation to productivity. The resulting number will still represent a substantial impact, but it will not necessarily imply a more realistic estimate.

■ **Field Sales Rep Turnover**: This ratio is simply the number of people leaving the field vs. the number of authorized positions. Every turnover event is costly to the company, whether due to internal transfer or people leaving the company. The implications of turnover include:

❖ Increased administrative costs

❖ Loss in revenue

❖ Loss in share

❖ Loss in delivered customer value

❖ Loss in available management time

Thus, turnover represents a double hit on productivity because there is a loss in revenue and an increase in costs. Sales automation applications can help to reduce the loss in revenue by providing call history, order history, and profile information that allows interim coverage either in person or by telephone. When a new person is hired, their learning curve will be reduced by having up-to-date information regarding the account, and with proper interim coverage, the customer should not feel abandoned due to the prior vacancy.

It can also be argued that unplanned turnover can be reduced by making the sales rep's position more reasonable to manage. Further, by having an automation system in place, it should be easier to attract desirable candidates.

The American Marketing Association reports that Northwestern Mutual Life Insurance Co. found that more than 90% of students used technology as a barometer to measure a company's health.[16] Automation can play a part in attracting top-quality college students.

During the past four years, Business Wire, a news wire service, has quadrupled its revenue. This achievement is related to their realization that to offer the best services and counseling for their clients, they had to minimize turnover. They developed a strategy that combines a substantial investment in training with benefits that escalate with service tenure.[17]

■ **Calls to Close**: This is a ratio that is used when dealing with long sales cycles and consultative sales processes. The issue here is really facilitating the buy cycle. The more value the salesperson can add to the buy cycle, the higher the likelihood of closing in fewer calls. Key to achieving fewer calls to close is the ability to answer questions faster and moving the process further with each call. Therefore, applications such as design capabilities, configurators, proposal generators, reference applications, and opportunity management software are essential to these situations. Reduction in the number of calls to close can be converted directly to the number of salespeople required to generate the plan numbers.

Moore Business Systems discovered that customers don't want just forms and traditional products; they want solutions to their information needs. Salespeople must now call on management-level positions in IS, marketing, and finance. Recognizing this and automating their system around these capabilities, they have experienced a double-digit improvement in sales force productivity and higher hit rates on sales calls.[18]

Revenue

Assumptions regarding revenue growth reveal a great deal regarding the potential of sales automation to leverage performance or indeed to become an essential strategic initiative. Revenue growth can be achieved through expanding business with existing customers, new products, and new customers or acquisitions. Since acquisitions can imply a wide range of issues, it will not be considered for this discussion; however, the reader is encouraged to explore this area thoroughly. Acquisitions can represent a need to merge sales forces, trade off accounts, use team selling, etc., all of which can be leveraged using automation applications.

Considering the other components of revenue growth, it is possible to construct some basic charts to segment each factor, as shown in Figure 12.1.

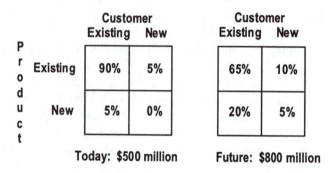

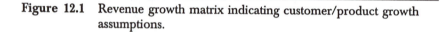

Figure 12.1   Revenue growth matrix indicating customer/product growth assumptions.

This matrix suggests a significant shift in source of revenue. Some basic questions that this change of mix raises are as follows:

- Is the new product replacing the existing product or is the product targeted at new areas of application (training and sales tools)?

- What is the source of the new business (lead management)?

- Are the new customers in the same industry or historical functional areas as existing businesses (training, sales tools)?

- Do the new products or targeted new customers represent a different competitive base (training, sales tools, competitive tools)?

- How does this focus match with competitive initiatives in the current customer base (sales tools, competitive database)?

- What programs can be expected from marketing (training, sales tools, decision models)?

The example in Figure 12.1 provides essential insight regarding the size of growth and the source of growth expected by the corporation.

Each component represents a unique set of capabilities and needs that can be addressed by a combination of sales automation applications. Note that the matrix could also be set up to compare revenue by channel, market, geography, etc.

From a strategic standpoint, providing applications that improve perceived risk associated with meeting these objectives will be well received by management. Meeting these objectives will mean hitting the revenue numbers. Meeting the numbers through increased productivity will reduce costs through cost avoidance (avoid hiring more sales reps to meet the $300 million growth in revenue). However, meeting the numbers while not achieving the desired mix could have dramatic consequences for this hypothetical company.

Margins

As described earlier, margin can be impacted by reduced costs, but the emphasis here is on the following:

- **Improved Product Mix**: An improvement in mix infers that revenue consists of a product mix that has higher margins on average. Achieving this type of shift requires awareness, motivation, and feedback. Sales force automation applications such as account planning, order entry, proposal generation, opportunity management, and electronic reports can all potentially play a role in this endeavor.

  Profit margins from new accounts are often much lower than those for subsequent sales. In addition, it takes an average of seven calls to close the first sale vs. three calls to close a subsequent sale with an existing customer.[19] In addition to the efficient use of sales resources, it is estimated that a 5% increase in customer retention can yield anywhere between a 20% to 100% increase in profitability.[20]

- **Discounting Price**: If left to their own devices, the majority of sales reps will discount price. This infers a lack of closing/negotiation skills or a lack of understanding regarding delivered value. Value, as defined in Chapter 5, relates to contribution to the customer's profitability and benefit as perceived by those influencing the buying decision. In this regard, the salesperson can add value to the process through insight regarding the supply market; design assistance and/or rapid turnaround on demos, samples, etc.; quick turnaround on pricing/quotes; and performance information. Related to price negotiations, applications that demonstrate life-cycle costs, assist in suggesting bundled pricing, etc. could be helpful. Thus, tools that shorten cycle time or deliver superior information (useful from the customer's perspective) will help to migrate the company from a vendor to a supplier, from a supplier to a preferred supplier, and from a preferred supplier to a partner. This transition means higher margins and lower operating costs.

The following statistics based on 3,424 surveys and gathered by VASS, a national sales training company, illustrate the problem:[21]

❖ Ninety percent of the salespeople offer customers a price cut without being asked. The reason for this high percentage is that they do not understand the benefits to the customer of what they are selling.

❖ Eighty percent of the salespeople refuse to close when the buyer is ready. As a result, 60% of buyers react angrily, feeling that their time has been wasted.

❖ Eighty percent of the salespeople were willing to accept a 90% rejection rate.

These are sobering statistics and demonstrate the merits of examining this area thoroughly.

Johnson Controls, a manufacturer of automated control systems, found that, ironically, salespeople who offer discounts in the hope of building strong customer relationships for the future are probably doing just the opposite. Company research shows that offering discounts actually tends to reduce customer loyalty. Some salespeople who have been repeatedly subjected to mistreatment will actually raise the price objection before the customer does, creating a discount situation where there doesn't need to be one.

Salespeople need to talk to the right people, who are charged with doing what's right for their company. These issues tie directly to training, sales tools (understanding and presenting value), and compensation (profit contribution and customer satisfaction).

■ **Customer Retention**: Customer retention is highly correlated with sales force productivity and account profitability. Therefore, this should be a key area for consideration. IBM Rochester reports that an increase of 1% in their customer satisfaction index equals a revenue opportunity of $257 million.[22] According to Reicheld and Sassen, a 5% increase in customer retention can yield a 20–100% increase in profitability.[23] Research conducted by the Forum Corporation indicates that 70% of the identifiable reasons why customers left typical companies had nothing to do with the product. This suggests that customer retention is a controllable variable.

■ **Marketing Allowances**: Effective use of marketing and promotional allowances is directly tied with margins. These allowances are common in a number of industries (e.g., plastics and consumer goods). **Effective** is a key operative word because it relates to accomplishing the intended purpose of the discount. Consumer-goods trade promotion allowances are intended to stimulate sales to the ultimate consumer, thereby encouraging trial purchase and brand switching. However, if the sales organization has a revenue target to hit, their objective will be to "sell-in" to retailers and wholesalers without a focus (accountability) on sell-through to the consumer. Without this focus, purchasing will be made on a forward-buy basis rather than a marketing-strategy basis. Clearly, a number of things have to take place. First, the sales force must share an accountability that is consistent with marketing goals, and they must be motivated to achieve these goals. Second, the sales organization must have appropriate tools to negotiate programs with the trade that are a win-win in that they serve both organizations' marketing strategy. Sales tools, opportunity management applications, negotiating tools, and electronic feedback are all potential solutions here.

- **Incentives**: Incentives can be part of an essential formula of successful field management, or they can be a destructive mechanism that encourages turnover and behavior that works against the organization and ultimately against the customer. Installing a sales automation system without careful consideration of existing incentive and bonus systems is akin to playing with a loaded gun. Learning International's 1990 sales force study showed that slightly over half of the sales executives interviewed said that their sales force's goals are based simply on revenue without taking profits into consideration.[24]

Costs

Based on the Moriarity and Swartz article, sales and marketing represent 15–35% of total corporate costs. With this leverage, it is hard to believe that substantial cost-reduction potential does not exist in this area.[25] Cost-reduction opportunities are readily apparent by charting the processes that touch the customer directly and/or are directly linked with the sales process. Some common examples are outlined below:

- **Sales Offices**: Field offices should serve a strategic purpose. If their role is solely one of providing an administrative oasis or as a depot for sales material, then their value added is questionable in the context of sales automation. It should not be a foregone conclusion that field offices will be closed; the issue must be approached from a value-added perspective.

  Published results of IBM's virtual office program are quite impressive. In one pilot area, sales reps averaged 6 hours less in the office, 1.8 hours less traveling, 8.1 hours per week working at home, and 2.8 hours more per week with customers. Another pilot indicated that revenue per rep is up 30% and sales cycle time has been cut 25%.[26] In a parallel action, Hewlett Packard hopes to achieve greater sales productivity, improved employee satisfaction, lower employee turnover, and reduced office space and parking requirements.

- **Expense and Vehicle Reports**: Field reports often must be reviewed by management and checked for accuracy and correct coding. Finally, the reports are entered into one or more systems. The result is long cycle time and wasted hours. In the interim, the salesperson may have to pay for the expenses out-of-pocket—a real negative. Electronic forms can eliminate virtually all of the reviews and data entry; thus, it is an easy win for the organization.

■ **Call Reports and Itineraries**: These processes are in wide use today. It is not uncommon to find field staff or even sales reps typing (typewriter) call reports or summaries. The timeliness and utility of this data approach zero. Obviously, electronic call reporting and reports distribution eliminate the extra steps in the process itself, but simply automating a call report system is like paving the cow's path—the potential should be much greater. This is a control vs. coaching issue that should be resolved before investing in a cannon to destroy a fly!

■ **Order Entry**: The order entry process is often subject to verbal translation of data and redundant handling of data, either in terms of transcription or correction. The result is often a process that increases delivery cycle times and adds to the total costs of the organization in ways that may not be apparent. Some common problems associated with order entry include:

❖ Incremental staff people required to key in and/or correct orders.

❖ Increased cash flow and inventory implications of delays in processing the order.

❖ Costs of correcting errors on the manufacturing floor or in distribution.

❖ Costs of expediting and lost manufacturing productivity due to the interruption of production cycles to correct problems or speed orders.

❖ Opportunity cost of salespeople in scramble mode correcting problems.

❖ Issuance of debits, credits, and eventual write-offs due to errors.

❖ Impact on the age of receivables when customers question invoices.

Certainly, one solution is EDI, but this does not work across the board. Applications like configurators and order entry can assist. Another key component of this issue is performance incentives and their influence regarding the quality and timing of the orders.

Order entry is a prime example of how quality of information can radically impact overall costs and cycle times. According to an article published in the *National Productivity Review*, up to 80% of the costs of poor quality on the manufacturing floor are attributable to functions outside of the manufacturing function, and many of these can be traced back to order entry.[27] The study further extrapolated that a 1% reduction in failure cost will yield a 4% increase in operating margins. Many organizations tend to view order entry as a data entry cost; this is far too narrow a focus.

■ **Training**: There is a distinct cost for undertraining (turnover, lost sales, low margins, etc.), and there are costs associated with inefficient training (high costs and opportunity costs). It has been said that training that is not closely aligned with meeting operational objectives is high-priced entertainment. The message here is that training needs to be an integral part of operational planning. Sales automation provides a number of options for supporting off-site training. Although computer-based training lacks the camaraderie of on-site training, it avoids the costs associated with pulling people out of the field. On the plus side, it affords the opportunity to conduct more focused training when people are on-site (e.g., team building). Also, there is a growing trend to engage the sales rep in defining his own training needs. Having a library of training materials could facilitate this process.

The effort of Tandem Computers, Inc. to develop a comprehensive electronic sales and training system for its 1,700 national and international field reps grew out of a company strategy to downsize its sales offices and mobilize its sales force. Reps spent too much time looking for information, and got different versions of information from different sources. Reps also used to receive "just-in-case" training, which essentially was a core dump. Now, the company offers JIT training with drill down capability. It includes a presentation creation module, a resource library, sales tips, positioning information, and demo scripts. Within 6 months the adoption rate was up to 70%. Sales reps use it 2.8 times per week. Warehousing, printing, and distribution costs are reduced by two-thirds. It saves the reps 2 hours per week and, overall, saves $2 million per year. Guides indicate how to prepare proposals and position against competitors.[28]

- **Turnover**: This topic was discussed earlier, but it has significant cost and revenue implications, as indicated below:

    1. Loss of management time in training an employee who leaves the company

    2. Pay given to the former employee while learning

    3. Costs of lost opportunities and customer dissatisfaction

    4. Recruiting costs and fees

    5. Management time spent in interviewing

    6. Cost of training the new employee

    7. Salary paid to new employee while learning

    8. Extra management time spent with the new employee

    9. Costs of mistakes

    10. Disruption suffered by the office

    11. Loss of knowledge of the business that only the departed person possessed

- **Forecasting and Planning Processes**: These processes often consume a disproportionate amount of field sales time, including field management. Paper-based systems have notoriously long cycle times, and the focus is often more on the numbers than the logic or assumptions. Even more disheartening is the fact that, in many cases, the numbers are not used for decision making or meaningful action. Sales automation can reduce the cycle time and effort associated with the processes, but there is great danger in simply automating a flawed process. Often, the organizational stakes are not well understood by the participants. The process should not be allowed to degenerate to a "my number vs. your number" mentality. Accurate forecasts can often have significant impact on inventory levels and manufacturing efficiency. Thus, the emphasis should be on collective input rather than comparative input.

- **Literature Fulfillment and Forms**: These are separate types of processes, but they have common cost ingredients. The process of creating and maintaining inventories of printed material is very expensive. When one includes damage and obsolescence, the costs are even higher. The resources handling these processes often are replicated throughout the organization; thus, the true cost of their existence is underevaluated. Therefore, centralized handling of requests and electronic versions of the material offer a vast improvement in quality, cycle time, and costs.

  Fixing errors in communication and forms processing can add up to 25% of the operating budget and staff hours.

- **Communication Costs**: Telephone and other communication costs are often very high. Electronic mail and the electronic distribution of reports often have a dramatic impact. The challenge is typically one of isolating the costs because they are often lumped into a single account.

- **Value Segmentation**: Market segmentation is often accomplished along sales volume and industry standards. Value segmentation is related to understanding and grouping accounts according to the opportunity for value added. The advantage of this segmentation is that it raises the question of the role of sales in providing that value added. Coverage is often an arbitrary choice without considering the benefit to the customer (which ultimately is reflected in the value to the supplier). This type of segmentation should drive deployment decisions and influence the choice of resource (e.g., tele-sales). The cost implications are obvious.

Properly designed tele-sales installations generate incremental sales productivity increases that range anywhere from 10–50%. Highly sophisticated programs have increased sales productivity in excess of 100%.[29]

Investment

- The PIMS (Profit Impact of Market Strategy) Principle states that superior quality at the top quintile earns an average ROI of 32% and a return on sales of 13%; the bottom quintile earns an ROI of 12% and a return on sales of 5%.[30]

- WIP turnover is the ratio of total sales to the value of WIP inventory. Labor productivity is estimated to increase by 35–40% with every doubling of WIP turnover through JIT or lean production methods that eliminate waste.[31]

Putting the Pieces Together

This chapter is like the proverbial double-edged sword. It has emphasized the significant costs and complexity of implementation while identifying the equally enormous potential for savings and competitive improvement. The thrust of this book is that organizations must understand both sides of the equation to be successful and that senior management must understand the human, technology, and business implications of implementation and continued support of the system. Only then can the project team assemble an implementation plan that will balance acceptance and learning rates of the field organization with the constraints of technology and the benefits derived by the company.

Endnotes

1. Louis A. Wallis, "Computer Based Sales Force Support," The Conference Board Report No. 953, 1990, 7.

2. Colleen Frye, "Sales Force Automation? Not Without Customization," *Client/Server Computing,* December 1994, 34–55.

3. David Hanaman, "How Sales Automation Is Changing the Organization," Culpepper and Associates, White Paper, 3.

4. Paul H. Seldon, "Calculating the Real Return of Sales Automation," *Sales Process Engineering and Automation,* March 1995, 9–16.

5. William C. Johnson and Richard J. Chvala, *Total Quality in Marketing* (Delray Beach, FL: St. Lucie Press, 1996), 213.

6. James W. Cortada, "Integrating a Baldrige Approach into a Sales District's Management System," *National Productivity Review,* Spring 1994, 318.

7. Tony Seideman, "Who Needs Managers?" *Sales & Marketing Management,* June (Part 2) 1994, 15–17.

8. Andy Cohen, "From the Field," *Sales & Marketing Management,* January 1996, 24.

9. Thayer C. Taylor, "It's Child's Play," *Sales & Marketing Management,* December (Part 2) 1994, 38–41.

10. Bob Francis, "Frito Lays a New IS Bet," *Datamation,* February 15, 1989, 75–78.

11. C. Welch and P. Geissler, "Measuring the Total Quality of the Sales Function," *National Productivity Review,* Autumn (1992), 517–31.

12. Tom Dellecave, Jr., "Getting the Bugs Out," *Sales & Marketing Management,* December (Part 2) 1995, 23–27.

13. George Stalk, Jr. and Thomas M. Hout, *Competing Against Time* (New York: The Free Press, 1990), 157.

14. Patrick Flanagan, "Getting the Paper Out of the Marketing & Sales Pipeline," *Management Review,* July 1995, 55.

15. Robyn Griggs, "Taking the Leads," *Sales & Marketing Management,* September 1995, 46–48.

16. Weld F. Royal, "The Profit Motive," *Sales & Marketing Management,* December 1995, 41.

17. Ginger Trumfio, "Keep the Lid on Turnover," *Sales & Marketing Management*, November 1995, 41.

18. Royal, "The Profit Motive," 43.

19. William O'Connell and William Keenan, Jr., "The Shape of Things to Come," *Sales & Marketing Management*, January 1990, 38.

20. Fredrick F. Reicheld and W. Earl Sasser, "Zero Defections: Quality Comes to Sales," *Harvard Business Review*, September-October, 1990, 38.

21. Geoffrey Brewer, "Survey: Sellers Giving Away the Store," *Sales & Marketing Management*, July 1994, 34.

22. Stalk and Hout, *Competing Against Time*, 158.

23. Reicheld and Sasser, "Zero Defections: Quality Comes to Sales," 38.

24. Kevin J. Cororon et al. *High Performance Sales Organizations* (Chicago: Irwin Publishing, 1995), 6.

25. Rowland T. Moriarity and Gordon S. Swartz, "Automation to Boost Sales and Marketing," *Harvard Business Review*, January-February 1989, 100–108.

26. Thayer C. Taylor, "Going Mobile," *Sales & Marketing Management*, May 1994, 96.

27. Welch and Geissler, "Measuring the Total Quality of the Sales Function," 517–31.

28. Robert L. Lindstrom, "Training Hits the Road," *Sales & Marketing Management*, June (Part 2) 1995, 10–12.

29. Richard L. Bencin, "First, a Solid Foundation," *Sales & Marketing Management*, June 1991, 99.

30. Robert D. Buzzell and Bradley T. Gale, *The PIMS Principles* (New York: The Free Press, 1987), 107.

31. B. Joseph Pine II, *Mass Customization* (Boston: Harvard Business School Press, 1993), 112.

CHAPTER 13

GETTING STARTED

A Long-Term Obligation

Sales force automation is a business decision to deploy and maintain a sophisticated networked computer system to support the sales efforts of the organization. This decision obligates the organization to a multi-phase project that will cover a period of 12–18 months and to a 6–8-figure investment. Implementing the project will require internal and external resources. It will pull salespeople out of the field, and it will subject the entire sales force to a distinct learning curve. The system will require continuous leadership and periodic investment to keep it current.

From an operating and competitive standpoint, the system should be expected to reduce administrative and process cycle time. Salespeople should be able to respond faster to the marketplace and add value to customers. Field management should be expected to better understand the marketplace and make sound decisions that result in more business at higher margins.

For the project manager or champion, the project means being on an emotional roller coaster, taking grief from the end-user group while trying to find solutions with the technical and support groups. It means fighting to save money in one area and turning around and spending more in another. In the end, there will be critics and advocates, but rest assured that you just completed a very complex process.

Gaining Senior Management Support

A question frequently asked at seminars pertains to gaining senior management interest in sales automation. The answer to that question is another question: What is senior management concerned about? Most senior executives will be interested in discussing opportunities to improve revenue, margins, and market share. Therefore, the starting place is to examine planning documents such as the 5-year plan and the annual report: What do they commit the organization to accomplish? How are the goals different from current goals? Speak with field sales management to gain a perspective regarding competition and what is needed to be effective with customers. As was discussed in Chapter 2, most companies operate within the framework of functional silos; therefore, it is important to understand where marketing, manufacturing, and product development are placing emphasis because, eventually, this will spill over to sales. How well is sales prepared for these events?

Financial people may be able to supply historical trend data for costs, revenues, margins, and head count. Historical trends need to be mapped against projected trends.

The next step is to gain insight regarding sales automation and its capabilities. There is no lack of seminars and other resources to gain a general appreciation of the technology and its capabilities. It should now be possible to highlight performance challenges and opportunities and link sales automation capabilities as a potential enabler. You may wish to form an informal team of interested parties and present the potential linkage as a group. In general, the charter to be sought is one that helps you build a solid business case. To do this, you will need assistance from marketing, sales, IS, and customer service. Members of engineering or quality management may be helpful from a methodology standpoint. The objective is to move the organization toward the completion of a needs assessment. It may be possible to map that out in one meeting, or it may require a series of steps.

Functional Description of Activity Content

To better understand the type of resources that need to be included on the project team, the phases of the project need to be understood in the context of functional needs. These functional activities can be segmented as follows:

- **Project Planning and Justification**: Within this segment, organizational needs and solutions are evaluated in the context of adding value to the customer and leveraging competitive capabilities. Therefore, the project needs representation from the organizations that directly interface with the customer. This could include marketing, sales, order entry, customer service, distribution, finance, etc. Since some of the work in this phase involves process mapping and problem solving, assistance from engineering and/or quality functions (group problem solving) may be helpful. Representation from IS is essential because the introduction of new technology requires their input and acceptance. Likewise, representation from finance is vital because the team will need help in cost justification and ensuring representation in key budget planning cycles. Buy-in from the financial community up front can save a great deal of time later.

- **System Development and Integration**: This activity embraces the design of the system, choice of vendors/platforms, and the interface with existing systems. Despite the fact that it sounds as though it is an IS task, there is a need for heavy end-user representation and buy-in. Thus, the project team must plan for the availability of field salespeople for this purpose.

- **Training:** The training implications of a sales automation project cannot be overemphasized; it represents significant change within the organization. Processes are likely to be changed, interfaces may be converted from voice to electronic text, old methods of networking may become obsolete, and new expectations may take their place. In addition, policies may have to be modified to reflect new responsibilities.

  Then, there is the technology itself; it represents a need to build new skills, disciplines, and a new vocabulary. The training plan must address all these areas plus develop knowledge and skill sets to operate the system. Though it is recommended that training for the pilot represent the same training environment and approach as the rollout, sometimes this is not possible. In this case, two training programs must be developed.

Finally, there is the question of on-going training of new salespeople. System training needs to be integrated into the new hire development program. Having a clearly identified strategy will help to minimize surprises and maximize investment in training resources and tools.

- **Deployment and Support**: This set of tasks pertains to the preparation of hardware and software prior to training. It also includes the development of support services, including the help line and equipment replacement/repair. Equipment preparation for the rollout is a major logistical event because the right equipment and software must arrive at the right location at the right time. Failure in this area is the classic "show stopper." Effective help-line support is critical after the system is in the field because the system essentially is the lifeline for the sales organization. Therefore, software/communications problems must be solved immediately.

- **System Administration**: Sales force automation systems are dynamic in nature. Customers are added, products change, accounts change in sales rep ownership, etc. The system must always be current because failure to do so will create a need for parallel capabilities (paper systems). When this happens, the system is not dead, but it is wounded. A system administrator(s) is essential to retain system relevance.

Project Structure

It is always difficult to speak in terms of absolutes, but the core membership of a project team should consist of 3–8 members. The **project manager** should be known and respected by the sales organization (current and former members). Membership ideally will consist of department-level management people representing sales administration,

IS, marketing, field sales, customer service, finance, training, and quality/engineering. By utilizing management-level people, the team creates an environment where policy issues and resource needs can be more adequately dealt with. Time commitments vary during the life of the project based on the role one is playing. What is perhaps more important is the *priority* one places on the project and its objectives.

The project must have a sponsor. That person must be at the senior executive level so that the effort is legitimized or "sanctioned." Most sponsors are vice presidents of sales and marketing, but a president, COO, or CEO could also be a sponsor.

Thus, at the beginning of the project, the project team will have the structure provided in Figure 13.1.

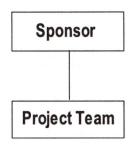

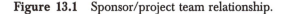

Figure 13.1   Sponsor/project team relationship.

As the project moves to the point of full approval and funding, it is recommended that the structure be expanded as follows:

- **Field Advisory Group**: Represents an ad hoc representation of field people from different areas and levels. The role of this group is to serve as a sounding board for plans, designs, and policies related to the project. They should represent a litmus test of acceptance, priorities, etc. as the field people will perceive it.

- **Executive Steering Committee**: The role of this group is to provide directional oversight for the project and to facilitate the work by assisting with policy decisions, resources, and/or visibility within the organization. Members of this group may include vice presidents within the same functional groups as the project team.

■ **Design Team**: Similar in structure to the Field Advisory Group but with a definite bias toward the end-user community. This group is responsible for input to the interactive design process that is used in creating screens for the system.

The resulting structure is recreated in Figure 13.2.

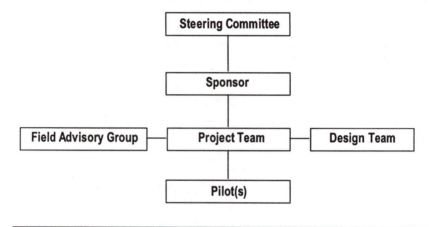

Figure 13.2   Overall project structure.

Final Comments

Structure and role definitions are of critical importance. Sales automation projects are high-profile endeavors, and there is substantial organizational power and credibility at stake. Thus, starting with a solid business case and business objectives is essential; without this frame of reference, the project will be subject to all types of pressures and winds that blow through the organization.

It may take more time and effort to set up this type of structure, but, in the end, commitment and resolve will win over elegance and speed.

CHAPTER 14

THE ROLE OF SENIOR MANAGEMENT

Virtually anyone who has experience with sales force automation recognizes that success in this endeavor is impossible without substantial support from senior management. Some may associate this need with the approval of funds and resources, and although this is certainly true, the role of senior management must be more expansive than this. Senior management has a specific set of roles and responsibilities that ideally should be understood up front. This chapter will outline areas that are uniquely within the province of senior management.

Danger Signals

This section is incorporated in this chapter because senior management must be cognizant of the risks involved with sales force automation and the importance of maintaining the right project team focus and environment. The heading "Danger Signals" has been chosen to reflect the consequences of flawed programs. Sales automation is a complex environment with many gotcha's but, at the same time, a wealth of opportunity. The following comments regarding surveys and other statistics available within the industry will reinforce the recommendations voiced throughout this book.

In an article entitled "Is Anyone Listening?", Thayor Taylor, a well-known freelance writer regarding sales force automation, reviews the results of a survey conducted by Culpepper and Associates. The survey indicated a fairly high percentage of customers who where dissatisfied with their sales force automation system.[1] The survey results segmented dissatisfaction as follows:

19% integration capabilities

14% inflexibility

14% incompleteness

11% difficulty in using the system

11% system bugs

The conclusions which can be drawn from these statistics are that the project team may have rushed to select software before considering the true nature of the sales process or that the evaluation of need never progressed over command and control issues. Difficulty in using the system may also reflect the quality of training, but also likely are "work arounds" that attempt to circumvent limitations in the system.

In a study conducted by Dell Computers, 60% of the respondents felt that they had met or exceeded their field automation goals. This same study identified two major barriers to success: (1) lack of senior management support (32%) and (2) field resistance (30%). These factors are really intertwined. Informed and involved senior management should insist on the design of the system to be driven by field users and that adequate training and change management be employed. Field users will also watch for signals from senior management relative to the commitment involved. If they conclude that management is committed, there will be a different attitude.

The Conference Board has conducted two surveys regarding sales force automation: the first one was done in 1986 and the second in 1989.[2] In the latest survey, about one-half of the companies reported a "serious" shortcoming with their system at one time or another. Obviously, without a definition of "shortcoming" or "serious," for that matter, it is difficult to be prescriptive; however, this terminology raises the specter of having a serious problem and not having senior management support! Entering into a sales automation project with the assumption that there will not be problems is not founded in reality; this is why the project team needs support and the infrastructure referred to earlier in this book. According to the report, a median level of 75% achievement of target was gained by those companies with completed (non-pilot) systems. Although 75% appears to be a high number, another way of looking at this statistic is that only 15% of the companies reached within 90% of their goal. Thus, the strike rate remains elusive.

In a survey conducted by International Data Corporation (IDC) of Farmingham, MA, which included 196 end-user departments and 206 information technology chiefs, 52% considered their systems to be up to expectation, 17% said it was too soon to tell, 2% said theirs were far below expectation, 21% said below expectation, and 8% said beyond expectations.[3] Some of the common causes for difficulty were reported as follows:

- Poorly defined rationale or goals associated with the project.

  Comments: This is the "if you don't know where you are going, any road will take you there" syndrome. Ill-defined objectives, such as automating before the competition does or "image" reasons, lack accountability and direction. An allied mind-set is that automation is something one must do, so let's accomplish it as inexpensively as possible.

- Overt technology orientation, where the focus of the project is on the sophistication of the technology rather than the business issues.

  Comments: Projects that emanate from IS or are subordinated to IS for implementation are virtually guaranteed to fail unless the IS organization is extraordinary in their sensitivity to end-user acceptance. This is not the fault of IS; the user organization has abandoned its responsibility to lead.

- A narrow focus on a few applications or a single solution for a problem may solve that problem but lead to a stand-alone system that cannot be expanded or integrated with other applications.

  Comments: Sales automation systems are dynamic. There is an on-going need for expansion and improvement. If this growth cannot be accommodated, interest will wane, and the viability of the system will be compromised.

■ A zero-based budgeting approach (each item must be justified incrementally) to sales automation is self-defeating.

Comments: There is nothing wrong with expecting business results, but the issue of automation is better approached from a whole rather than the sum of the parts. Long-term success is going to be a function of use of the system; therefore, it is wise to lead with applications that will make sense to sales reps and thereby make them more likely to want to use the system. These same applications may or may not provide the organization with the highest near-term return.

■ Inadequate assessment of initial investment and operating costs will drive organizations to shortcut system performance or dilute services.

Comments: The result of these decisions is to encumber the end-user community with inefficiencies that cloud the value of the system. Given the learning curve associated with mastering a new system, many users simply give up or otherwise exhibit behavior that sabotages the system.

■ Senior management must be overt in terms of stating expectations regarding the use of the system and the anticipated results.

Comments: Consequences either need to be inferred or explicitly stated. Despite the hype of designing systems that everyone is going to love, make no mistake—the system represents change, and some people will test the resolve of the company to make it happen.

■ Designing and implementing systems with a "control" orientation will result in resistance and sabotage.

Comments: From the beginning of the industry, "Big Brother" issues have been discussed. It cannot be emphasize strongly enough that the system must leverage the sales effort and deliver value to the customer to be effective. Even under these conditions, it is not uncommon to hear about Big Brother. When this occurs, it is important to discuss the concerns openly; there have been cases where Big Brother related to a layer of management that sales reps felt uneasy about.

■ Attempting to "fix" processes with automation is analogous to paving the cow path.

Comments: There is no magic in the technology; if garbage is placed in the system, garbage will come out, albeit faster! This is frequently apparent in forecasting systems. If one merely automates the process without doing anything to improve the quality of the input, the results will be useless data generated in a fancy format.

■ Ignoring incentive and bonus systems that negatively affect field behavior which is critical to system acceptance will essentially undermine any attempt to institutionalize the system.

Comments: Performance-based systems and related policies must be evaluated up front; otherwise, there is significant risk that they will impact results in some undefined manner.

Jim Dickie, a consultant with Insight Technology Group, Boulder CO, looked at 175 projects that were launched in the early 1990s. He found that only 32% were on time, 36% came in within budget, 12% achieved their goals, and 28% of managers expressed satisfaction with the eventual product.[4]

The Gartner Group is unique within the systems consulting business in that it has a group that is dedicated to research regarding sales force automation. This group has come to the conclusion that the first wave of sales force automation has essentially failed. The primary reason is an inordinate focus on the reduction of costs as opposed to improving the quality of the sales interface. In conference presentations, the Gartner Group refers to the art and science associated with sales automation. This is indeed the nature of the project; it represents a unique amalgam of strategy, innovation, change management, and technology. For this reason, sales automation cannot effectively be implemented as a bottom-up initiative.

It would be very hard to leave this section without providing some positive hope. These statistics are indeed sobering. The primary issue with sales automation is that there tends to be an uncoupling of technology with the business. Despite its name (an unfortunate misnomer), sales force automation is not about implementing a technology. The broader issue is how one improves the ability of the organization to deliver value to the customer. Sales automation as a technology offers a host of enabling technologies and applications to facilitate this effort, but allowing the technology to come into focus too soon will jeopardize the initiative. Methodology helps in this regard, but overall leadership is essential, and that is why this section was placed in this chapter. Senior management must be actively engaged in the effort and ensure that the project team does not get pulled off from the strategic objectives of the initiative.

The Phoenix Principle

The Phoenix is a mythological bird that pulls itself from the ashes to fly again. Similar to the Phoenix, there have been a number of projects that were dismal failures but which became successful when placed on the right track. It is important to realize that a failure is not a life sentence for the organization. The following represents but a few of such projects.

In an article in *Forbes,* Hewlett Packard, Pitney Bowes, John Fluke, and Ingersoll Rand are noted as having systems that failed. The following were considered contributing factors to the failure:

- Overselling by the vendor

- Covering up mismanagement

- Underestimating the commitment and the time required to reach desirable levels

- Making the project a science project

- Overreacting to a dip in productivity before seeing results

- Introducing technology for technology's sake

- Failing to take ownership of the system (sales force)

- Failing to be motivated to succeed (salespeople)

- Failing to recognize the continuous building nature of the automation process

Armstrong World Industries, Inc., Building Products Operations Division, implemented sales force automation in 1990. It proved to be a failure because it offered nothing to help sales with the sales process. In 1995 the company had another go at it, but this time the company consulted its sales reps to find out how technology could increase their productivity. They have selected a specific selling methodology: (1) the ability to connect sales reps with each other as well as with the corporate office and (2) ease of use.

John Fluke Corporation, a manufacturer of electrical testing equipment, failed at sales force automation primarily because they tried to put too much into the system at once.[5] They did not involve enough people in the design; the assumption was that they knew what the field needed. This was compounded by significant delays by the vendor. The net effect was increasing resistance by the field organization at the same time that senior management was becoming impatient with the pace of the project. Ultimately, the project was canceled and would have remained a dead issue. However, in a dramatic exercise of courage and leadership, one of the original team members revisited the field and began to pull together the elements of the project that truly worked for field sales (system was in pilot). Based on a new plan, senior management agreed to invest another $500,000 in a reduced scope project that is being driven by the field organization.

In the late 1980s, Upjohn, the pharmaceutical company, embarked on a number of pilot systems with consistent negative results. Essentially, the problem was that IS staff was designing systems the sales organization did not relate to or own. When leadership was transferred to the sales organization, the project turned around and remains successful.

Understanding Requirements and Committing to Make It Happen

The development, installation, and rollout of a sales automation system requires 12–18+ months. Other applications can be added to the system at reasonable intervals thereafter. Each interval requires learning and lost field time for salespeople, so there is a balance of value to the organization vs. opportunity cost. Once a system is installed, it requires (1) the on-going support of a "champion" to ensure that the right things are happening, (2) an administrator(s) to keep the system current, (3) IS staff to monitor and maintain operations, and (4) service staff to handle the help line and replace broken equipment.

For large projects, there may be 20–50+ people working on some aspect of the project; therefore, it is virtually certain that outsourcing of tasks is essential. The selection of a project manager is a critical decision. The choice sends an immediate message to the organization regarding how important this project is to the success of the organization. Other members are also important, but the project manager is key. This person must be a strong advocate for the field organization yet be pragmatic in terms of being able to trade off capabilities or timing for critical end-user needs.

Senior management must be committed to provide a vision for the sales organization and communicate that vision effectively. From the very beginning of the investigation of sales automation, senior management must communicate with the field organization the status and direction of the project. As more detail becomes available, the message must be expanded to setting proper expectations.

Any sales force automation project is going to change the way people work, their habits, and the manner in which things get done. This represents **change** in the lives of the field people and the support people they interface with. Whether people see this change as being positive or negative does not alter the fact that their lives and the way they operate are going to be different. The word for change in the Chinese language is a compound word meaning **danger** and **hidden opportunity**. This compound word is very relevant to sales automation. If the change component is ignored, it can have a negative impact; however, if handled correctly, it can provide unexpected dividends. Change management experts have defined stages that people must go through to assimilate change; this process is directly analogous to stages people experience when grappling with a terminal disease. The challenge of all this is that senior management must be steadfast in terms of purpose and commitment while being sensitive to the change process. It has been found useful to instruct field management regarding this behavior process because it is counter-intuitive. What appears to be resistance or negative behavior is sometimes merely a person working through the change. Ultimately, the completion of the process is dependent on the commitment of senior management. Even when field sales receives significant benefits through the automation system, there may be people who resist. At some point the message has to be made that this is the manner in which the company will do business—other options are not acceptable.

Lastly, senior management must be committed to proper training and support of the system regardless of budget constraints. If this commitment cannot be made, then a serious case can be made for not proceeding.

Support of the Project Team

Sales automation projects are somewhat like a roller coaster. The initial high of getting organized and starting the project is often followed by a distinct emotional drop when the enormity of the challenge becomes apparent. Senior management should be aware of this and continue to encourage the team at the low points and celebrate with the team at the highs.

The project team must be chartered to define the needs of the organization from a competitive and business perspective. This type of perspective should be possible within one or two months given reasonable staffing. More time than this points to implementing the wrong level of detail or becoming hung up on unnecessary issues. At this point, the project team should be able to articulate basic needs and opportunities. For example:

- Field turnover is 25%.

- It takes two weeks to generate a proposal.

- All pricing deviations must be reviewed by a committee that approves 95% of the submissions.

- Three people spend all their time checking expense reports.

- No one can clearly define the sales process.

- At this stage, there should be an absence of concern about technology.

Leadership

Although *leadership* is a common management term, it conjures up different images in each person's mind. Since this section deals with a specific message, the following distinction is established regarding leadership and management:[6]

- "Managers are people who do things right."

- "Leaders are people who do the right thing."

It is important to maintain sight of what the organization is trying to create for itself through the project. No matter how well planned and researched a project has been, surprises and trade-offs are inevitable. The question is, what perspective is used in making the decisions? If the perspective is building the organization and ensuring that key operational or competitive capabilities are achieved, then this may be contrary to short-term project goals. Senior management must be sensitive to this and work with the project team so that decisions which impact long-term success are not compromised due to pressures on schedule or project cost.

Although it should be expected that project members exercise both management and leadership traits, senior management must be ready and willing to address hard issues. For example:

- Dealing with policy issues that have been long-standing but are not relevant or are counterproductive.

- Making decisions about staffing issues.

- Making decisions about redeployment of field resources.

- Investing in formal change management when conditions warrant it.

- Doing things right up front (see comments below).

- Replacing project members if required.

- Managing risk.

The project team must feel accountable for the management of the project. They need to have the support of senior management to bring issues to the table that are critical to the integrity of the system. Sales automation is a classic case of a "pay me now–pay me later" trade-off. Consider the implications shown in Figure 14.1.

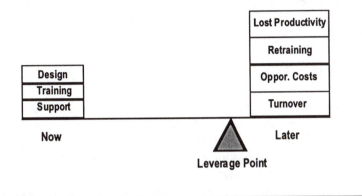

Figure 14.1   The cost trade-off between doing things right up front vs. paying later.

The now-or-later issues are among the toughest to deal with regarding sales automation projects. Variances in project cost and timing are painfully obvious, yet the consequences of shortcutting these costs are substantial. The problem is that they are typically not associated with the project; rather, they get muddled in operational costs. When push comes to shove, where does the "leverage point" rest? The project team needs to know that senior management is going to support doing the right thing!

IS vs. Business Project Management

The history of sales automation is punctuated with standoffs between IS and the end-user community. The reason for this is that the early systems tended to be built on a specific platform. If the end users liked the interface but IS did not like the platform, the battle lines would be drawn. On the opposite side of the coin, when IS takes the leadership from the start, the results are seldom acceptable because there is a tendency to dictate to the end-user community vs. getting them involved. In reality, the business and IS sides of the house must cooperate and develop a perspective so that each function can appreciate the trade-off between capabilities, standards, and overall cost of operation. To achieve the best environment to accomplish the transition from business needs to technology solution, information technology must be viewed as a vehicle for gaining strategic advantage and the IS organization as a vehicle for delivering value. With this mindset, there is a natural transition of logic and shared responsibility for delivering the project. Senior management must help assume this same posture so that conflicting agenda's do not occur.

Providing a Future

When the rollout is complete, senior management must provide a home for project members and ensure a viable future for the system. Continuing support for the system requires an end-user advocate (champion) as well as a continuing commitment on the part of IS to support modification and expansion of the system. Care must be exercised in handling these resource assignments because the decisions speak to the importance of the system and the level of support and acceptance received.

Endnotes

1. Thayor C. Taylor, "Is Anyone Listening?" *Sales Process Engineering and Automation,* June 1995, 18–19.

2. Louis A. Wallis, "Computer Based Sales Support," The Conference Board, Report No. 953, 1990.

3. International Data Corporation, "Sales Force Automation Pays Off," *Sales & Marketing Management,* December (Part 2) 1994, 9.

4. Jeffrey Young, "Can Computers Really Boost Sales?" *Forbes,* August 28, 1995, 90.

5. Malcolm Flescher, "Out of the Ashes," *Personal Selling Power,* July/August 1993, 37.

6. Warren Bennis and Burt Nanus, *Leaders* (New York: Harper and Row, 1985), 21.

CHAPTER 15

LOOKING AHEAD

Trends and Management Concerns

In a survey of 1,450 executives conducted by Gemini Consulting, Morristown, NJ, managers rated being organized around customer requirements and being flexible in meeting market conditions as the top 2 of 34 capabilities.[1] Major findings from the study include:

- The need to transform the organization on a continuous basis (regeneration).

- Operational excellence is no longer considered a source of sustainable competitive advantage.

- Businesses are not prepared for the future. The study found major gaps in performance, trust, and effectiveness between senior management and the organization.

- Businesses are less globally minded than expected.

One can conclude from these findings that the ability to change and adapt to the marketplace are key concerns. Organizations need both the strategy and the organizational environment to accomplish this.

According to research conducted by Mercer Management Consulting, in Lexington, MA, reengineering and downsizing have made organizations leaner but not richer. In a survey of 180 U.S. executives, 94% of them said that growth is a top priority.[2]

Peter Senge, author of *The Fifth Discipline,* cites a Shell study that indicates that one-third of the Fortune 500 companies vanished during the period 1970–1983.[3] The study further identified a small number of companies that survived through their ability to explore new business and organizational opportunities that created growth. Senge expanded on this approach and refers to it as the "Learning Organization." In this model, the leader is responsible for building an organization where people continually expand their capabilities to shape the future.

In a similar concept, Robert Tuite, managing partner at The Innovation Strategy Group, Inc., a Rochester, NY, consulting firm, suggests that companies build their management processes around the goal of being a systematic innovator. This implies looking ahead at quality and flow of potential profit generation and the development of choice based on market facts and logic as opposed to emotion and politics.

These trends and concerns are likely to play out in the following ways:

- Organizations will develop regenerative strategies that emphasize flexibility and reduction of cycle time.

- There will be an increased focus on industry transformation. As outlined in Chapter 2, basic business designs are taking on the life-cycle characteristics that previously were associated with products. Not recognizing an industry transformation can be an organizational disaster.

As outlined in the comments of Senge and Tuite, organizations must adapt to competing for opportunity vs. market share.

What this implies is a change in perspective. The concept of the enterprise must be expanded to include customers and suppliers. Suppliers must truly understand the customer franchise. Fundamental to these strategies is the sales organization. It is time to invest in the sales function and approach it as a source of value added and as a competitive weapon.

The future of the enterprise depends on this capability; the lesson from the 80s is that you cannot cost reduce yourself to competitive advantage or profitability. The issue is not one of productivity but, rather, one of strategic necessity.

Management Tools vs. Strategy

Over the past 20+ years, there have been a series of management initiatives, including group incentives, productivity, quality, and reengineering. Each of these initiatives had positive attributes but tended to get caught in the confusion between the tools vs. the philosophy. There is always a component of management that will seek "silver bullets," hoping that the tools will represent a total solution. This is seldom the case.

Sales automation sometimes takes on this same mind-set. Organizations seek to "automate" before the competition without an understanding of the competitive threat or advantage. These installs are seldom successful because success is never really defined. There should be a very strong parallel between TQM, reengineering, and sales force automation. Each of these initiatives should truly start with the customer. Without this discipline, each of them is equally likely to get off track or take on a life of its own.

The closest concept to a philosophy in sales force automation is the "ten do's" relative to implementation. This book has positioned sales force automation as an operational tool that is intended to facilitate the delivery of value to the customer.

It is perhaps time for the industry to redefine itself. The technology that pertains to field salespeople really relates to field-based customer service people and other professionals who operate with minimal office presence. In this respect, it is the mobility of the individual rather than the function that is important. Bringing all these pieces together would suggest the following concept:

Mobile Solution Systems (MSS): Networked systems technology that supports the value-added efforts of field organizations and the process of continuous improvement.

Value as Strategy

Value has been used throughout this book as a customer-oriented focus that helps to break the tendency of organizations to think in terms of internal criteria. If used properly, it has the unique feature of capturing the desires and needs of the customer in terms of product and services. Value encapsulates the attributes of cost, quality, and service. It is key, however, to utilize a customer profitability definition vs. a got/cost perspective (what did I get/what did it cost?). The distinction represents a quantum leap in thinking; profitability encourages the supplier to understand how the customer competes. Customer profitability encourages "foresight" and understanding of the forces that will shape future industry structure. Got/cost will drive strategic thinking into four-wall metrics.

Value, as compared with other initiatives, is reflected below in Figure 15.1.

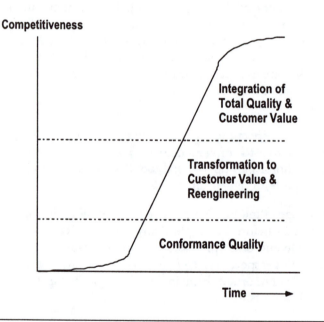

Figure 15.1   Competitive impact of the customer-value strategy.

Value is an effective mechanism for making the customer "real" to the organization. When integrated with quality, the combination of value/

quality management will drive the organization naturally in the direction of adaptation and learning. Thus, the strategy has a market focus that will drive organizations toward competitive advantage.

The Industry

The sales force automation industry consists of services, software, and hardware. From a historical perspective, the entire industry has grown faster than its early pioneers expected. A contributing reason for this was the rapid growth of laptop technology which provided enormous power and utility in a very small footprint and at a very affordable price. This rapid growth in technology, however, represented a "catch"; the software had to keep up. Ultimately, many software suppliers could not maintain their value relationship, and they have ceased to exist. The message here is to keep the operation at a size at which value can be maintained.

This implies that suppliers will need to operate in application niches and adopt standards so that their applications can be effectively linked to applications provided by other sources. Transport mechanisms and systems integration are likely to be provided by other suppliers. In order to support second, third, and fourth generation installs, end-user organizations are going to need multiple application systems, with perhaps some of these applications being custom developed. Applications that can be linked together to form a seamless interface on a value-based price will be the winners.

This arrangement will drive the service component of the industry. With the emphasis on outsourcing and downsizing, most end-user organizations will not be interested in "make" options or in systems integration; therefore, these services will be in high demand.

Similarly, if systems represent an integration of many applications, then third-party training and help-line resources will be in high demand because no software developer will have the critical mass to support the services. The service providers will need to hone their methodologies and develop tools that allow them to customize deliverables in a time-compressed and on a high-value basis.

In summary, the industry is likely to evolve toward niche-oriented application developers and system/services integration. For end-user organizations, this will significantly complicate the vendor selection process. It also reinforces the need to have a well-established business direction before embarking on a technology search. The sources of risk are substantially higher in this environment; sound management is not a luxury—it is a necessity.

The Ultimate Competitive Weapon

The ultimate competitive weapon is people! The real issue for any organization is how to tap into the true capabilities of its people. Every year the Gallup Organization teams with *Sales & Marketing Management* magazine to identify the best sales forces in the United States. The criteria used in the selection process are as follows:

- Accuracy: Does the organization maintain the detail of transactions and manage them?

- Availability: How accessible are the salespeople?

- Credibility: Confidence and respect given to the salespeople as reflected by the following:
  - Are they viewed as resources by customers?
  - Do they build confidence regarding the company's capability and competence?
  - Do they perform their job with excellence?

- Partnership: Are their objectives and actions consistent with the needs of the customer?
  - Do customers seek sales reps to discuss ideas?
  - Do the sales reps help customers meet goals?
  - Does the knowledge of the sales rep make it difficult for the company to be replaced?

- Trust: Are the sales reps consistent in their follow-up and commitment?

- Discovery: Do the sales reps provide ideas to customers, and do customers seek them out for advice?

These are all people issues. Technology can obviously assist, and, certainly, technology can provide better linkage between company/rep/customer, but sales reps must be trained, and incentives and business philosophy must be consistent with excelling in the above areas.

The Decision to Invest

In their book *Sustaining High Performance,* authors Stephen Haines and Katie McCoy provide a valid call to action: "The best way to guarantee your future is to create it yourself."[4] Whether automating for the first time, replacing a failed system, or entering the fourth generation of automation, the issues remain the same. How does technology fit into the framework of competitive strategy? Take the time necessary to truly invest in the sales function and establish a competitive beachhead that is built on people and technology. This does not imply a massive study, but it does suggest ensuring that the right pieces are in place so that you can maximize your potential for success.

A number of companies have pulled themselves out of the ashes of failed installations to go on to implement successful systems. This demonstrates the resiliency of the organization. Success is possible if you approach the issues from the right perspective and demonstrate a commitment to the people and to achieving the desired results.

An investment in an automation system should be viewed as a continuous investment. The system must be maintained and the people supported. It is very likely that other features will need to be added over time. The system will also need to be replaced every four to five years. These replacements should be viewed as an opportunity to enhance competitive position, and each install should become easier, provided that each project team learns from the previous one.

Endnotes

1. Eileen Davis, "What's on American Managers' Minds?" *Management Review,* April 1995,14–20.

2. Ibid.

3. Peter M. Senge, "The Leader's New Work: Building Learning Organizations," *Sloan Management Review,* Fall 1990, 7–23.

4.   Stephen G. Haines and Katie McCoy, *Sustaining High Performance* (Delray Beach, FL: St. Lucie Press, 1995), 115.

BIBLIOGRAPHY

Band, William A. *Creating Value for Customers.* New York: John Wiley, 1991.

Barabba, Vincent P. *Meeting of the Minds.* Boston: Harvard Business School Press, 1995.

Bencin, Richard L. "First a Solid Foundation," *Sales & Marketing Management,* June 1991, 99.

Bennis, Warren, and Burt Nanus. *Leaders.* New York: Harper and Row, 1985.

Berrigan, John, and Carl Finkbeiner. *Segmentation Marketing.* New York: Harper Collins, 1992.

Berry, D. "Marketing Mix for the 90's Adds an S and 2 C's to 4 P's," *Marketing News,* December 24, 1990, 10.

Blattberg, Robert C., and John Deighton. "Interactive Marketing: Exploiting the Age of Addressability," *Sloan Managment Review,* Fall 1991.

Blessington, Mark, and Bill O'Connell. *Sales Reengineering from the Outside In.* New York: McGraw-Hill, 1995.

Bogan, Christopher E., and Michael J. English. *Benchmarking for Best Practices.* New York: McGraw-Hill, 1994.

Brewer, Geoffrey. "Survey: Sellers Giving Away the Store," *Sales & Marketing Management,* July 1994, 34.

Burris, Roger. *Technotrends.* New York: Harper Business, 1993.

Buzzell, Robert D., and Bradley T. Gale. *The PIMS Principles.* New York: The Free Press, 1987.

Callahan, Madelyn R. "What Customers Want," *Training & Development,* December 1992, 31–36.

Campanelli, Melissa. "Reshuffling the Deck," *Sales & Marketing Managment,* June 1994, 83–90.

——. "What Price Sales Force Satisfaction?" *Sales & Marketing Mangment,* July 1994, 37.

——. "Can Managers Coach?" *Sales & Marketing Management,* July 1994, 59–66.

——. "Sound the Alarm," *Sales & Marketing Managment,* December 1994 (Part 2), 20–25.

Campanelli, Melissa, and Thayer C. Taylor. "Meeting of the Minds," *Sales & Marketing Managment,* December 1994, 83.

Cespedes, Frank V. *Concurrent Marketing.* Boston: Harvard Business School Press, 1995.

Champy, James. *Reengineering Mangement.* New York: McGraw-Hill, 1995.

Churchhill, Gilbert A., Jr., Neil M. Ford, and Orville C. Walker. *Sales Force Management.* Boston: Irvin, 1993.

Cohen, Andy. "A New Surgical Tool," *Sales & Marketing Management,* September 1994, 49–50.

——. "Right on Target," *Sales & Marketing Management,* December 1994, 59.

——. "From the Field," *Sales & Marketing Management,* January 1996, 24.

Corcoran, Kevin J., Laura K. Petersen, Daniel B. Baitch, and Mark F. Barrett. *High Performance Sales Organizations.* Chicago: Irwin, 1995.

Cortada, James W. *TQM for Sales and Marketing Management.* New York: McGraw-Hill, 1993.

——. "Integrating a Baldrige Approach into a Sales District's Managment System," *National Productivity Review,* Spring 1994.

Crego, Edwin T., Jr., and Peter D. Schiffrin. *Customer Centered Reengineering.* New York: Irwin, 1995.

Davis, Eileen. "What's on American Managers' Minds?" *Management Review,* April 1995.

Dellecave, Tom, Jr. "Getting the Bugs Out," *Sales & Marketing Management,* December 1995 (Part 2), 23–27.

Deming, W. Edwards. *Out of the Crisis.* Boston: Massachusetts Institute of Technology, 1982.

De Rose, Louis. *Value Selling.* New York: American Management Association, 1989.

Dimancescu, Dan. *The Seamless Enterprise.* New York: Harper Business, 1992.

Drucker, Peter F. *Tasks, Responsibilities, and Practices.* New York: Harper & Row, 1973.

Earls, Alan R. "Brave New World," *CIO,* June 1, 1995, 86.

Fillon, Mike, "Keep on Trucking Yellow," *Sales & Marketing Management,* June 1995 (Part 2), 17–19.

Flanagan, Patrick. "Getting the Paper Out of the Marketing & Sales Pipeline," *Management Review,* July 1995, 55.

Fleschner, Malcolm. "Out of the Ashes," *Personal Selling Power,* July/August 1993, 37.

——. "Training That Lasts," *Personal Selling Power,* March 1995, 32–33.

Francis, Bob. "Frito Lays a New IS Bet," *Datamation,* February 15, 1989, 75–78.

Frye, Colleen. "Sales Force Automation? Not Without Customization," *Client/Server Computing*, December 1994, 34–55.

Gale, Bradley T. *Managing Customer Value.* New York: The Free Press, 1994.

Goldman, Steven L., Roger N. Nagel, and Kenneth Preiss. *Agile Competitiors and Virtual Organizations.* New York: Van Nostrand Reinhold, 1995.

Goodman, John. "The Nature of Customer Satisfaction," *Quality Progress*, February 1989, 37.

Griggs, Robyn. "Taking the Leads," *Sales & Marketing Management*, September 1995, 46–48.

Haines, Stephen G., and Katie McCoy. *Sustaining High Performance.* Delray Beach, FL: St. Lucie Press, 1995.

Hamel, Gary, and C. K. Prahalad. *Competing for the Future.* Boston: Harvard Business School Press, 1994.

Hammer, Michael, and James Champy. *Reengineering the Corporation.* New York: Harper Business, 1993.

Hammer, Michael, and Steven A. Stanton. *The Reengineering Revolution.* New York: Harper Business, 1995.

Hanaman, David. "How Sales Automation Is Changing the Organization." Culpepper and Associates White Paper.

Harrington, H. James. *Total Improvement Management.* New York: McGraw-Hill, 1995.

Hayes S., and W. Harley. "How Buyers View Industrial Sales People," *Industrial Marketing Management*, 18 (1989), 73–80.

International Data Corporation. "Sales Force Automation Pays Off," *Sales & Marketing Management*, December (Part 2), 1994, 9.

Johnson, H. Thomas. *Relevance Regained.* New York: The Free Press, 1992.

Johnson, William C., and Richard J. Chvala. *Total Quality in Marketing.* Delray Beach, FL: St. Lucie Press, 1996.

Lindstrom, Robert L. "Training Hits the Road," *Sales & Marketing Managment*, June (Part 2) 1995, 10–12.

Magrath, Allan J. *Zero-Defect Marketing.* New York: American Management Association, 1993.

McCloskey, Larry A. *Selling with Excellence.* Milwaukee: ASQC Quality Press, 1995.

Moad, Jeff. "IS Satisfies the Customer," *Datamation*, October 1, 1993, 79.

Moore, Geoffrey A. *Crossing the Chasm.* New York: Harper Business, 1991.

Moriarity, Roland T., and Gordon S. Swartz. "Automation to Boost Sales and Marketing," *Harvard Business Review*, January-February 1989, 100–108.

Morse, James F. "Predators and Prey: A New Ecology of Competition," *Harvard Business Review*, May-June 1993

Naumann, Earl. *Creating Customer Value.* Boise: Thomson Executive Press, 1995.

Naumann, Earl, and Patrick Shannon. *Business Horizons,* November-December 1992, 44–52.

Neusch, Donna R., and Alan F. Siebenaler. *The High Performance Enterprise.* Essex Junction, VT: Oliver Wight Publications, 1993.

O'Connell, William, and William Keenan, Jr. "The Shape of Things to Come," *Sales & Marketing Management,* January 1990, 37–41.

Peters, Tom. *The Tom Peters Seminar.* New York: Vintage Books, 1994.

Pine, Joseph, II. *Mass Customization.* Boston: Harvard Business School Press, 1993.

Pittiglio, Rabin, and Todd McGrath. "Why Companies Fail at TQM," *IIE Solutions,* May 1995.

Primozic, Kenneth, Edward Primozic, and Joe Leben. *Strategic Choices: Supremacy, Survival, or Sayonara.* New York: McGraw-Hill, 1991.

Reicheld, Fredrick F. and W. Earl Sasser. "Zero Defections: Quality Comes to Sales," *Sales & Marketing Management,* January 1990, 38.

Reilly, Tom. *Value-Added Selling Techniques.* Chicago: Contemporary Books, 1989.

——. *Value-Added Sales Management.* Chicago: Contemporary Books, 1993.

Retchfeld, Barry. *Personal Selling Power,* September 1993, 26–33.

Robert, Michel. *Strategy Pure & Simple: How Winning CEO's Outthink Their Competition.* New York: McGraw-Hill, 1993.

Royal, Weld F. "On-Line at the Prudential," *Sales & Marketing Management,* June 1994, 42.

——. "The Profit Motive," *Sales & Marketing Management,* December 1995, 41.

Santosus, Megan. "Pursuing the Perfect Pitch", *CIO,* October 1, 1994, 80.

—— "New Value Systems," *CIO,* June 1, 1994, 33–34.

Seideman, Tony. "Who Needs Managers?" *Sales & Marketing Management,* June (Part 2) 1994, 15–17.

——. "A British Revolution," *Sales & Marketing Management,* August 1994, 115.

Seldon, Pual H. "Calculating the Real Return of Sales Automation," *Sales Process Engineering and Automation,* March 1995, 9–16.

Senge, Peter M. *The Fifth Discipline,* New York: Doubleday, 1990.

——. "The Leader's New Work: Building Learning Organizations," *Sloan Management Review,* Fall 1990, 7–23.

Slywotzky, Adrian J. *Value Migration.* Boston: Harvard Business School Press, 1995.

Stalk, George, and Philip Evans. "Time Based Competition," *Harvard Business Review,* March-April, 1992.

Stalk, George, Jr., and Thomas M. Hout. *Competing Against Time.* New York: The Free Press, 1990.

Taylor, Thayer C. "SFA: The Newest Orthodoxy," *Sales & Marketing Management*, February 1993, 96.

——. "Going Mobile," *Sales & Marketing Management.* May 1994, 96.

——. "It's Child's Play," *Sales & Marketing Managment*, December (Part 2), 1994, 38–41.

——. "Is Anyone Listening?" *Sales Process Engineering & Automation Review*, June 1995, 18–19.

——. "Sales Automation Cuts the Cord," *Sales & Marketing Management*, July 1995, 110–115.

Thomas, Philip R. *Competitiveness Through Total Cycle Time.* New York: McGraw-Hill, 1990.

Tomasko, Robert M. *Rethinking the Corporation.* New York: American Management Association, 1993.

Treacy, Michael, and Fred Wiersema. "Customer Intimacy and Other Value Disciplines," *Harvard Business Review*, January-February 1993, 84–93.

——. *The Discipline of Market Leaders.* New York: Addison-Wesley, 1995.

Troiano, Domenic, and Michael Troiani. "Profile: Data General's High Technology Customers Benefit from Telesales," *Telemarketing*, November 1994, 38–44.

Trumfio, Ginger. "For the Love of a Laptop," *Sales & Marketing Management*, March (Part 2) 1995, 31–34.

——. "Keep the Lid on Turnover," *Sales & Marketing Management*, November 1995, 41.

Usilaner, Brian, and Michael Dulworthy. "What's the Bottom Line Payback for TQM?" *Journal for Quality and Participation*, March 1992, 82–90.

Wallis, Louis A. "Computer Based Sales Force Support." The Conference Board Report No. 953, 1990.

Walton, Mary. *The Deming Management Method*, New York: Dodd, Mead, & Co., 1986.

Welch, Cas, and Pete Geissler. *Bringing Total Quality to Sales.* Milwaukee: ASQC Press, 1992.

——."Measuring the Total Quality of the Sales Function," *National Productivity Review*, Autumn 1992, 517–531.

Whiteley, Richard C. *The Customer Driven Company.* New York: Addison-Wesley, 1991.

Young, Jeffrey. "Can Computers Really Boost Sales?" *Forbes*, August 28, 1995, 85–88.

Zangwill, Willard I. *Lightning Strategies for Innovation.* New York: Lexington Books, 1993.

INDEX

IRRATIONALITY IN
INTERNATIONAL
CONFRONTATION